TEACHERS UNDER THE MICROSCOPE

A review of research on teachers
in a post-communist region

DANA HANESOVÁ

authorHOUSE

AuthorHouse™ UK
1663 Liberty Drive
Bloomington, IN 47403 USA
www.authorhouse.co.uk
Phone: 0800.197.4150

Reviewers: Bronislava Kasáčová, Alena Seberová, Charl Wolhuter

Published by AuthorHouse 06/25/2016

ISBN: 978-1-5246-3389-9 (sc)
ISBN: 978-1-5246-3388-2 (hc)
ISBN: 978-1-5246-3387-5 (e)

Print information available on the last page.

Any people depicted in stock imagery provided by Thinkstock are models,
and such images are being used for illustrative purposes only.
Certain stock imagery © Thinkstock.

This book is printed on acid-free paper.

Because of the dynamic nature of the Internet, any web addresses or links contained in
this book may have changed since publication and may no longer be valid. The views
expressed in this work are solely those of the author and do not necessarily reflect the
views of the publisher, and the publisher hereby disclaims any responsibility for them.

CONTENTS

Appendices

PREFACE

The beginning of the third millennium has become a strange 'cradle' for new-born babies. The world has been facing various new forms of violence and cruelty. The role of educators in raising the new generation has become more and more emphasized. In addition to parents, teachers have the greatest opportunity to influence the relationships of the young generation toward other people and toward their environment. The teachers' role is to positively influence the character development of each student in their class, as well as to assist them in developing into well-educated citizens who are capable of thinking intelligently and critically in their society. On the other hand, teachers are expected to become agents of school reform, and ideally, agents of change in the social climate as well.

So – what does it mean to be a teacher? What kind of profession is it? Which competencies, knowledge and skills are typical for a professional teacher? What are his/her characteristics, ambitions, joys and struggles? What is the position of teachers in society? What is necessary to become and continue to be a high-quality professional teacher? These and similar other questions have been the foci of manifold research studies on teachers for decades.

The same is true in previously communist countries. Researchers in Central and Eastern Europe have conducted extensive research on teachers and the teaching profession. Though this research was limited because it was embedded into the core of educational sciences during communist times, recent educational reforms in post-communist countries have sparked an intensive discussion related to the social status of teachers and their professional competencies.

The reason for writing this book can be introduced by the words of Webber and Liikanen (2001): "In research on post-communist transformations, however, education is still only seldom afforded the attention it deserves … It is most important to recognize, e.g., the role of education in influencing patterns of social relations within these countries … In the context of a post-communist transformation, these [listed educational] issues acquire an additional degree of complexity, as any discussion of such notions as equality and individual choice are heavily tainted with perception of the legacy of the communist system" (p. 2).

This study presents results of an investigation focused on teachers, their education, status, profession, and professional activities in Central Europe before and after the fall of the Iron Curtain in 1989. Senior educationalists and researchers divide the history of education in this region into two distinctive periods, using the fall of the communist regime of 1989 as the dividing line (e.g. Maňák in Czechoslovakia, 2005, p. 8).

As most of the research studies in this region, especially those from the pre-1989 times, were published in native Slavic languages, I decided to produce an overview of research on teachers accomplished in this region in both periods in English. Not being a native speaker of English, I realize my vocabulary is rather limited, but in spite of that I hope the information in this book might be understandable and useful for serious researchers.

Though I was born and educated in socialist Czechoslovakia, I am aware of the danger of creating a black-and-white picture of our story. To avoid it, I drew on a variety of resources. But the fact is that when speaking about the period before 1989 especially, it is impossible to avoid some subjectivism from our side. It is now possible to evaluate only that partial information that appeared in officially censored documents. Only limited amounts of analysis and evaluation were completed in the sphere of education sciences before 1989. Texts that were forbidden to be published or which were distributed only among small groups of professionals have a diminishing chance to be taken into consideration or to contribute to the formation of a more complex view, because many of their authors have died already. A significant educational scientist, Mareš (2010) suggested making an attempt of a systematic study of the past as soon as possible.

These are the reasons I approach the topic of this book with high respect. An exhaustive study would require a large team of authors. I decided to use some available data to at least paint a draft of the picture of how research on teachers looked before 1989, as well as early after the democratic revolutions. Thus this publication might serve essentially as a reference book.

My purpose is not to spread negative ideas about how harmful Marxist education, science, and research was, even though the negative signs of it were so obvious. Instead, my attitude is that of scientific humility, and my goal is to share research on the historical development of teachers in order to understand the current situation in post-communism better and to establish grounds for useful international comparison.

I would kindly ask the reader to take the data on research as examples of research, not as an exhaustive catalogue of all research on teachers. Also, I ask the reader to view my interpretation as an attempt to give an approximate account of the research situation in Czechoslovakia and other Eastern Bloc countries before 1989.

Key words: research, teachers, post-communist, history, comparison, feminisation, recruitment, professional activities, 'Iron Curtain'

Contact

Assoc. Prof. PaedDr. Dana Hanesová, PhD.
Faculty of Education, Matej Bel University
Ružová 13, Banská Bystrica, Slovakia
dana.hanesova@umb.sk

INTRODUCTION

More than a quarter of a century has passed since the 'Fall of the Iron Curtain' – the collapse of communist regimes in Central and Eastern Europe (1989 – 1990). The previous era of 'building communism' (1948–1989) has often been characterized as a period of ideological indoctrination of education (Š. Švec, 2002, p. 78). In the communist totalitarian regimes, education shared the fate of the whole society (Maňák, 2013, p. 386). The teaching profession was particularly monitored, more than other professions, as the aim of educating young people toward adopting a communist worldview was one of the priorities of the communist governments. Activities of teachers were restricted and centrally directed by the respective communist governments. Key educational documents reflecting the educational policy during this period, e.g. the Resolutions of the Communist Party on education, or textbooks for future teachers, or even textbooks for children extensively confirm this assessment.

Teachers faced this pressure in three different ways. Most of them adapted to the conditions of their work, some of them actively cooperated with the Soviet regime in order to have a successful career, and a few of them became dissidents and emigrated from the Soviet Bloc (Průcha, 2010). In spite of the heroism of various courageous individuals – teachers, pedagogues and educational researchers and their criticism of the system – out of necessity the aims of education and the educational research policy remained subordinated to the ideology of the Soviet communist regime. The criticisms of educational professionals include but are not limited to the educationalist conference in Prague in 1956 in which Pavlik criticized the thoughtless copying of the ideas of Soviet pedagogy (according to Taborsky, 1961, p. 514), and Polish author, Jersak, who, in 1957, criticized negative aspects of the centralized management of Polish schools.

Of course this included vast limitations of educational research – the range of research issues and publishing of them, the use of certain research methods, and/or quoting from a restricted number of selected resources. Otherwise, the person making the quotation might have been blamed for opening him/herself to 'positivism', or some other 'heretical' approach connected to so-called 'bourgeois science'. Thus, the educational research had to remain at the service of propaganda.

After 1989, one of the first steps of the newly established parliament was the abolition of the leading role of the Communist party and its ideology. Soon after these radical political changes, the ideas of the humanistic educational paradigm with its new view on teachers and their autonomy filled the vacuum, which was created after cancelling the Soviet Marxist educational paradigm. The ideas present, particularly in Western education, spread quickly through the post-Marxist region, finding fertile ground in bottom-up initiatives of excited teachers in the 1990s. Since that time, numerous organizational changes in school legislation and educational reforms have been gradually been implemented in both the various educational systems and in the preparation of teachers in post-communist countries in Central Europe. However, this process has been far from easy, and it has constantly faced various challenges and turbulence that I will refer to at several points in this book.

The turn toward democracy included opening the way to freedom of educational research, including research of the teaching profession. Though potentially it could have started right after the democratic revolutions, it took almost a whole decade for the new research paradigm to be established. Lecrercq commented that even then it was impossible for a researcher outside of a post-communist country to form a deeper opinion on the subject of teachers and research on teachers because of the newness of the situation and the shortage of detailed statistical data needed to make international comparisons (1996, pp. 87–100). Much more precise data on the socio-professional structure of teachers were needed, e.g. on the number of teachers in various stages of education, male/female ratio, feminization of teaching profession, salaries and financial attractiveness of teaching profession, levels of teacher education, prestige of the teaching profession in comparison with other professions, age structure of teachers, length of their practice, number of teaching hours, and the workload of teachers.

The teaching profession in Central European democracies was vigorously shaken in the beginning of the new millennium by the mandatory decision of the Bologna process and the new national educational Acts to divide teacher education (further TE) programmes at universities into two discontinuous/or only formally connected levels – Bachelor and Master degrees of TE. In Hungary, Slovakia and other countries, this caused a violent disruption in the systematic professional development of teachers' professional key competencies (Kosová, 2011, p. 56 and ff.).

In Hungary, unstructured teacher education was re-introduced in 2013 (Gyorgyi, 2015). In Slovakia, voices calling for the reintroduction of an undivided system of TE have been intensifying each year but, at the time of writing, without a response (for instance, see the *Statement of the Association of Deans of Teacher Education Faculties ...,* 2011). According to Kosová, an undivided system would strengthen the importance and the state support for the teaching professions and would raise their social status (2011, p. 57). An example of this effort was the project *Transformation of University Teacher Education in the Context of the Reform of Regional School System,* carried out by University of Matej Bel and fourteen other Slovak TE faculties in 2011, supported by the representatives of the Ministry of Education, Science, Research and Sports. It analyzed and evaluated the impact of the Bologna process on TE institutions with a focus on researching and analyzing the current crisis in TE and searching possible solutions. The project team prepared a new conception of university TE that would reflect the new needs of educational practice.

In the Czech Republic, the current accreditation process will lead to a decision whether or not to fulfill the desire of teaching faculties for the return of non-structured preparation for the teaching profession, which is similar to a medical doctors' profession (2016). Several research studies, for instance, on students' motivation to study at either structured or non-structured teacher studies, are currently being carried out (Mazáčová, 2013).

In Slovakia, after a turbulent period of several legislative interventions of the state, which was mainly concerned with the external conditions of good teaching, there are still many areas in the educational system that need radical improvement. This is in spite of proclaiming its support to the growth of quality of education. One of the most vivid of them is the professionalization of the teaching profession itself. There is a need to step out from shallow discussion and move toward genuine interest in the vital role of teachers as agents of social change in this generation's education. In Slovakia, experts in educational theory for pre-primary and primary levels consider the issue of developing teachers' professionalism, including the standards of their performance and the ethical codes of their profession, to be crucial societal issues in Central European society (Kasáčová & Kosová, 2006; Kosová, 2011, p. 11). Research on the growth of teachers' professional competencies, on their professional knowledge, and on their ability to engage in self-reflection, has become a main focus of teacher education at the Faculties of Education in Slovakia.

It is time now to focus on the developmental trajectory of research on teachers during the period of transition, comparing research before and after to discover what changed and to what extent it changed in comparison to the previous period. Furthermore, it is also important to identify the trends of teacher research in this region. What is the current situation regarding the teaching profession, especially regarding research on teachers? On what aspects of the teaching profession does research on teachers in post-communist democracies focus? Is there any resemblance between the trajectory of research on professional activities of teachers in these transitioning countries and nations in the Western block?

The aim of this book is to try to answer at least a few of the above-listed questions. The author of this book will start with a general *diachronic* overview of the wider educational context in both historical periods – before and after the democratic revolutions in 1989. She will present the main foci of research on teachers in both periods as well as noting what research methods were used most frequently. Most of the examples of research presented are from the Slovak Republic (from where the author comes), but in quite a few cases, the book reports on research from other post-communist countries, especially the Czech Republic. In a few sections, the author also indicates possible comparisons with Western countries. The aim of this *synchronic* overview is to discover overlapping trends of research on teachers, e.g., in the area of expectations from teachers and their responsibilities and competencies, their workload, and especially their daily practices.

The book consists of four main parts. In the first part of the introduction, the characteristics of pedeutology, a science studying the teaching profession, and of its pedeutological research from the point of view of a Central European researcher are described. Here also, the author presents the main line of the book – her three-dimensional approach to the research on teachers in the post-communist region, namely diachronic, synchronic and methodological.

In the second part, the story of research on teachers in Czechoslovakia, similar to other Central European countries, in the period 1948–1989 is presented. Besides historical comments, it includes brief overviews of the topics of the research and research methods used under the Soviet regime.

The third part shows the features of the transition period in the Central European region right after the democratic revolutions in 1989. Again, categories of research areas and research methods are listed, this time with a less comprehensive account of the rapid growth of pedeutological research in this region. Specific attention is paid to account for professiographic research throughout both of the periods.

In the last, fourth chapter, we present three research topics in more detail, with the main results of research in those areas. The first of these is research related to the motivations for entering teacher training and forms of recruitment to study at a teacher education faculty; the second focuses on the issue of feminization among teachers. Finally, results from a comprehensive, international, comparative research project on teachers' professional activities and professiograms are presented.

The study refers to several types of resources:

- Studies in several Slovak and Czech educational journals (published in the Slovak and Czech languages) from both before and after 1989;
- Lists of research grants awarded to university researchers;
- Selection of original research studies, anthologies, proceedings, resolutions of the Communist Party, monographs on education from both before and after 1989 recommended by other university Czech and Slovak educationists.
- Some paragraphs of this study have already been presented and published in partial studies by their author Dana Hanesová (2014 & 2015) with the agreement of their editors and publishers.

Notes:

The phrase **'Fall of the Iron Curtain'** was chosen purposefully to indicate the importance of political changes in Central and Eastern European countries in 1989 because that date divides the historical (including educational) continuum clearly into historical epochs – before and after the fall of the Soviet communist regime. The use of this phrase in this study expresses the quest to find evidence of changes in education that researchers have claimed to have happened in the former Eastern Bloc after the 'Fall of the Iron Curtain'.

One more explanation about dividing the overview of research into two periods is required. Research on teachers before 1989 was much less extensive and less systematic than research since 1990. This difference is indicated in the text of this publication, concretely in the names of main units, naming the research in the first period as *research on teachers*, and research in the second period as *pedeutological research*, set into a more thorough theoretical framework.

Linguistic note:

The word *pedagogika* has been used in the publication several times. In continental Europe, including Slovakia and the Czech Republic, this term – *Pädagogik* in German, *pedagogika* in Slovak and Czech, *pedagogia* in Polish, *pedagógia* in Hungarian, etc. – has much wider meaning than "the method and practice of teaching" as it is often understood under the word *pedagogy* described in Anglo-American countries. It seems that the best equivalent in English language would be *educational science(s)* (e.g. according to Průcha, 2002; Š. Švec, 1988). The reason of the use of the term *pedagogics (pedagogy)* in spite of the fact that it is not so widely used in the Anglo-American studies is a simple need to recognize the authenticity of the national/regional particularities of the countries we are focusing on in this study, including the linguistic expressions used in them.

1

What is pedeutological research
(research on teachers)

1.1 Pedeutology and its research paradigms

The process of the transformation of education in post-communist countries in transition brought along a discussion about the status of teachers. Experts have paid increasing attention in post-communist countries to **pedeutology** – the theory of the teaching profession, its core content, its societal function, and the preparation for this profession (Kasáčová, 2004, pp. 5–13). Pedeutology has had quite a long tradition in Central Europe. Though its primary function was to set some normative requirements for teachers, it has become a progressively developing educational science.

Similar to other sciences, pedeutology has its own range of sub-topics. It studies the objectives, preconditions and conditions of professional activities of the teaching profession as well as mental and social demands and expectations from the teacher, his/her personality, education and job performance. Thus, pedeutology is concerned with topics, such as these (Kasáčová, 2004):

-   Pre-service teacher preparation (its philosophy, content, the structure of curriculum, the ratio of theory/practice);
-   Teacher's biodromal career (all its stages: the phase of choosing the career, and of an experienced teacher, life-long learning of teachers, risks of the profession, burn-out);
-   Professional activities of teachers (pedagogical thinking, communication, competence, professiography);

- Historic development the teaching profession;
- International comparisons via statistics and other data on teachers;
- Typology of teachers (according to the level of school, subjects, psychological characteristics, etc.);
- Social and economic status of teachers;
- Morals of the teaching profession;
- Pedeutological research (Kasáčová, 2014).

To gradually deepen and develop its own level of knowledge, pedeutology cannot exist without serious **pedeutological research**, i.e. research on teachers and all the issues associated with this profession (more about relevant theories and approaches in Lukas, 2007 & 2008; an overview of research in the Czech Republic by Lukášová, 2009).

Perhaps as a remnant from the previous historical period, there has been a tradition in many post-communist countries of taking a normative (prescriptive) approach to what teacher competencies and performance should look like. This may be based on normative theories and created ideals of normative models for the professional profile of teachers. The position of a normative science is, to some extent, quite natural for pedeutology, a theory defining the norms for teachers' preparation, actions, and behavior in the classroom. During the communist history of Central European countries, however, the normative role of pedeutology and its research was over-emphasized (especially during the political period of normalization, in Czechoslovakia in the years 1968–1989 when the norms for the teaching profession were based primarily on political criteria, and only secondarily on professional criteria) (Kasáčová, 2004, pp. 8–9).

Around the beginning of the new millennium, due to the criticism of such models and other manifold challenges, pedeutological researchers in the transitioning countries realized the need to begin their investigations with descriptions of the more or less complex educational reality in schools. The international educational policy context specified the capabilities, competencies, qualities and skills of teachers (Lisbon Strategy, Bologna Declaration, etc.). Though this has been a natural process for the developed democratic countries, researchers from the transitioning countries had to understand the need for serious changes in the direction of their research methodology. They had to shift from researching only what was suitable for the state ideology and confirming some theoretically-prescribed features of the educational system, to first investigate the reality (*descriptive research*), then to analyze, explain and evaluate the acquired data (*explanatory and evaluative research*). Only then did they dare to recommend and experiment with some new proposed ideas and conduct genuinely *prescriptive research* based on the analysis of real facts, needs, etc., and not on political decisions as typically happened in the previous period. In several areas, researchers have begun to explore unknown, new, and so far unsearched variables and their relations (*exploratory research*), e.g. the researchers investigating the influence of transformation of school curricula (in Slovakia as well as other countries – Porubský, Kosová et al. 2014). This is an example of how pedeutology started to develop its role of an exploratory and explanatory science in the previously socialist countries as well.

All of the above-mentioned research paradigms require their own adequate **research methodology**, which in the past – as in most countries – was predominately quantitative. After the concept of truly free, democratic investigation developed in the 1990s, the volume of qualitative (or predominately qualitative) research began to grow. This trend was confirmed by several studies that tried to quantify the ratio between them (Gavora, 2004). Chapters 2 and 3 describe in more detail the methodological approaches of both periods (before and after 1989).

Before focusing further on the context of pedeutological research, it is important to point out that research has always played a crucial role in the development of the educational sciences – throughout both described periods. As the descriptions in chapters 2 and 3 will show, there have always been researchers interested in the precise investigation of educational reality and some of them have written substantial theses on the issue of educational research. A team of Slovak educators led by Š. Švec produced an exhaustive publication on methodology used in the educational sciences (1998 & 2nd edition in 2009). To demonstrate the complexity, multi-dimensionality and seriousness of their approach to educational research, including research on teachers, here is one of their key ideas, related to ***the purpose of research***. Any educational research, including research on teachers, is to be perceived only as an element (often the first) that contributes to the progress of educational science. This happens provided that the research results are taken into consideration and are actually used in the further process of developing the theory or putting it into practice. The implementation of research results has to be reflected on, re-evaluated, and, again, implemented in schools. Already in the 1980s, the necessity of interdependence of research and development of new procedures/products based on the research discoveries, was pushed forward by means of centralized, governmental instructions, aiming at accelerating scientific and technological progress and the economic welfare of society (Š. Švec, 1998, p. 47). It seems that due to the decentralization that occurred as one of the transformation steps in the transitioning countries, the idea of this cyclic, actually spiral process of development using research results has been neglected and must be stressed again.

1.2 Multi-dimensional approach to categorization of research

Each national/regional educational system has its own 'biography' which means that education – similarly to other spheres of civic life in each country – has been molded not only by the outside societal (international) macro-context, but primarily by a set of internal factors, very specific for a certain country/region or a community (mezzo- and micro-context). As several studies on specific educational issues indicate, certain phenomena such as the history of the nation/region, legislation, economic development and social welfare, ethnic and religious structure of population, culture and traditions, and the history of education, seem to be the main factors influencing the development of regional educational systems and the status of teachers (e.g. Schreiner et al, 1995 & 2002). The overall approach to education and to the educational sciences, including pedeutology and its research, has been shaped by a specific synthesis of these constituents.

The framework of the study is the flow of the nation's historical and political development. Thus, the *first* lens through which pedeutological research will be studied, is a historic – *diachronic* angle of view, investigating two politically distinct historic periods (during and after the collapse of communism in Eastern and Central Europe). This idea of such a comparison is based on the fact that "education cannot be taken out of context of social events... From this perspective the (past) period is divided into two very different parts – the dividing moment is the fall of the communist regime in 1989". (Maňák, 2005, p. 7).

The *second* dimension of the following comparison concentrates more closely on two intertwined issues, characterizing each line of research – *research problem* and *research method* as ways to discover the core of the problem and, respectively, the solutions. With the exception of the fourth chapter, this publication does not go into details or an analysis of all topics represented in individual research studies. It only mentions their main outlines in order to create a broader view of the approximate themes of research, which could serve its evaluative and comparative purposes. The same applies to comments on the research methodology in different periods. A simple division into the main research paradigms – (predominantly) quantitative or (predominantly) qualitative – is pointed out, supplemented by an overview of the main research methods or techniques.

Finally the *third* dimension of the publication are the indications (treated in less detail and more implicit than explicit) of a *synchronic comparison* of the research situation in parallel existing countries and their educational research. Synchronic research on teachers, for example, allows us to see that the present low status of teachers, limited motives of choosing the teaching profession, low teachers' self-image, and "growing uncertainty of teachers' professional identity" are present in most post-communist countries. An international team of researchers under the management of Pusztai & Ceglédi (2015) investigated the typical post-communist climate as the source of the worsened situation. They pointed to the fact that "the countries of Central and Eastern Europe have obviously to cope with the burden of the long-lasting effect of the ideological pressure on teachers since the middle of the last century" (p. 7). The concluded that ongoing distrust and suspicion, mainly between teachers and parents, was a particularly negative influence.

The result of synthesizing all these dimensions (Scheme 1) should lead to a retelling, as comprehensively as possible, of the story of the increase in pedeutological research in specific post-communist countries, mainly Slovakia but with some comparison to other countries.

Scheme 1: Three dimensions of research on teachers (Dana Hanesová)

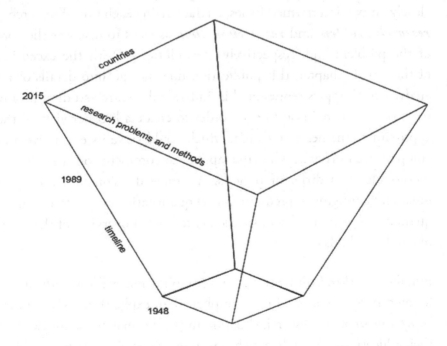

1.2.1 Chronology of research studies
throughout historical periods

Three recent historical facts have had a radical impact on the development of modern pedeutology and its research in the former socialist countries (including Slovakia):

- The end of the 1980s: *Perestrojka* and massive demonstrations of citizens in most Central and Eastern European countries resulted in the collapse of the Soviet communist regime which took control of these countries shortly after WWII (1948). Well-supported by the broader context of political changes in the Soviet Union and other socialist countries in Europe, in November 1989 the *Velvet Revolution* took place in Czechoslovakia, in the next 1–2 years the Marxist state ideology was abolished;
- The beginning of the 1990s was characterized by the separation of states formerly based in federations (e.g. the *Velvet Divorce* of Czechs and Slovaks) and the *constitution* of new democratic states (e.g. formation of the Czech Republic and the Slovak Republic in 1993). The process of transforming the political system with its first multiparty elections, recreating a market economy, and reorienting foreign policy was initiated. The schools were claimed to be free from any ideology and doctrinaire teaching methodologies. One impact of these changes was the opening new opportunities for more critical approach to educational practice and genuine educational research;
- In 2004 all four Central-European Visegrad countries (the Czech Republic, Hungary, Poland and the Slovak Republic) plus four other post-communist countries (Estonia, Latvia, Lithuania, and Slovenia) joined the European Union.

The development of the teaching profession in these countries, as an integral part of the state educational system, proceeded in proportion to the conditions in which it has taken place. According to Hargreaves

2000; Walterová, 2002; Kasáčová, 2004; Kasáčová & Cabanová, 2009, compared to the development of the teaching profession in Western Europe, the development of the teaching profession and of research on teachers in the Central European region can be described in four stages:

- *The pre-professional stage* of the teaching profession in most European countries in the first half of the 20th century: Teaching as an occupation was regarded more as a mission than as a profession: Teachers in this epoch were mostly 'half-educated', with low social status and very poor salaries. Being a teacher in this period could be marked as a semi-profession. This was a period of research focused predominantly on the learners. Only later did researchers' interest shift to investigating teachers.

- *The stage of professional autonomy* in the beginning of the second half of the 20th century: The differences started to occur. In the developed European countries, this phase was typical with its democratizing reforms of the education system, raising the quality of pre-service preparation of teachers which became a pre-condition for becoming a professional teacher. The improved social status of teachers was evidenced by raising the quality of teacher preparation and teachers' wages. Teachers became relatively 'autonomous professionals'. In Czechoslovakia and other Soviet Bloc countries, in spite of promising beginnings of a growing emphasis on teachers' professionalism, e.g. via the Decree of the president Beneš in 1945 enacting compulsory tertiary level of teacher education, ideological indoctrination became a hindrance to the growth of teachers' autonomy. So in spite of the fact that several authors significantly contributed to the development of pedeutology before 1989 (in Czechoslovakia e. g. Špendla, Janoušek, Baláž, Višňovský – according to Kasáčová, 2009, p. 35), concepts such as *professional autonomy* were fully accepted and started to be implemented in practice only after the change of the political system in 1989. The same can be said about the professional autonomy of educational researchers.

- *The stage of crisis of professionalism and de-professionalization* started in Western Europe in the 1970s. It was stirred in society by criticism of teachers related to their inability to adapt their teaching properly to the growing volume of knowledge. All the detailed standards of curricula, strict inspections, and testing contributed to the growth of a strange climate called *de-professionalization*. In the eyes of society, the status of teachers was decreasing. Research at this time focused on new approaches to efficient pre-graduate teacher preparation. The cumulative impact of the criticism of teachers was the decrease of attractiveness of the teaching profession in comparison to other new professions. Elaboration of educational standards and of evaluation systems enabling rigorous international comparisons also added to the crisis. In the transitioning countries, several signs of crisis in the teaching profession remain evident even to in the present time. These signs of crisis in the teaching profession have been investigated and confirmed recently by a group of researchers from three post-communist countries (Poland, Slovakia and the Czech Republic). Thanks to the Visegrad Fund, they were able to carry out a parallel research project, demonstrating an ongoing crisis related to the ageing of teachers, feminization among teaching staff, a lack of qualified teachers, low salary and low attractiveness of the profession, and rising demands placed on teachers (Engler, Kovács & Chanasová 2014b, pp. 145–146).
- *The stage of neoprofessionalism of the teaching profession,* since the 1990s, is characterized by its search for a new professional identity. The developed countries adopted the concept of 'knowledge society' that would consider its schools and teachers to be the key force of its development. This new trend has been reflected in educational reforms, including reforms of teacher education aiming to transform the teaching profession and to build teachers' professionalism on the reflection of societal needs. According to ATEE Conference (Association for Teacher Education in Europe), in 2002 reforms of teacher education

were taking place or being considered in all developed countries. A significant degree of attention has been devoted to the process of teachers' initiation into their profession. According to the research of Kosová – a Slovak expert on the influence of reform on the teachers in most post-communist countries in transformation, including Slovakia, the signs of the period of neo-professionalism have not been evident yet (2011, p. 8).

1.2.2 Categorization of pedeutological research according to its focus and method

'Research on teachers' is a very broad term. Since 1989, hundreds of research studies would fall into this category. As in case of other multifaceted, complex social phenomena, development and trends in pedeutological research can be described via categorizations of their main research areas or research foci. Czech (Spilková, Blížkovský, Průcha, etc.) and Slovak (Kariková, Kasáčová) experts have developed several categorizations which are going to be referred to and combined with the previous two dimensions.

The teaching profession can be researched according to its various dimensions. For example:

- Dimension of development of the teaching profession (pre-professional, professional autonomy, crisis, 'deprofessionalisation', and neoprofessionalism);
- Dimension of professionalism in the teaching profession;
- Personal dimensions of the teaching profession:
    - Motivation to enter the teaching profession – the decision to become a teacher;
    - Personal aptitude to become a teacher;
    - Cognitive presuppositions;
    - Ethical dimensions;

- Expert dimension and its developmental phases (biodromal perspective – Charts 1–3).

To present the overall picture of the boom in research since the 1990s in Slovakia and the Czech Republic, we decided to apply a pragmatic classification of basic categories to which the various research projects completed in these countries belong (suggested by Kasáčová, 2004, Slovakia):

- Research on pre-graduate teacher education – It is a very rich category with many research studies. Yet, it has been decided that for the purposes of narrowing the extent of this study, it would be considered as a different topic.
- Research on teacher career – This broad category consists of several sub-categories:
    - Choice of teacher education;
    - Motivation to study;
    - Becoming a novice teacher;
    - Lifelong teacher education;
    - Experienced teachers;
    - Threatening factors of teacher education, burn out;
    - Specific phenomena of teaching profession: relations, feminization, satisfaction.
- Research on individual teachers' activities;
    - Research of teachers' pedagogical thinking;
    - Pedagogical communication and its aspects;
    - Teacher capabilities and competence;
    - Professiography – analysis of specific professional activities of teachers, their workload – tracing changes in the profession and the origins of various phenomena;
- Research on historic development of teaching profession:
    - Comparison of teacher education, social status – documents;
    - Development of the teaching profession;
    - Development of pedagogical opinions on the teaching profession;

- Development of schools of teacher education;
- Development of curricula for teacher education;
- Historiography;
- National and international comparison of teachers;
- Typology of teachers:
  - According to type and level of school;
  - According to personal characteristics;
  - According to characteristics of various school subjects;
- Social and economic status of teachers;
- Ethics of teaching profession;
- Other important research topics:
  - Teacher's attitudes;
  - Relations between teacher and student;
  - Requirements for teacher competence;
  - Teacher preparation in various countries;
  - Evaluation of teacher work;
  - Psychological characteristics of teachers.

Probably the most frequent point of view used for categorizing pedeutological research is the so called '*biodromal' approach*. A Slovak researcher in this area, Kariková (2015), explains the origin of this concept from biodromal psychology. Kariková researches personal values and the meaning of life, or ways of self-realization, and studies them through all the consecutive phases of life. By "*biodromal view* the concept of personality development as a process of permanent change taking place, with the potential for growth, enrichment and change, even into adulthood and old age is understood" (p. 11). Its main focus is on changes that have manifold results. Applied to pedeutological research, it means that its categories are going to be distinguished according to the *phases of teacher's career,* for example, in the following way:

- *Research in the motivational phase* during which a person decides to become a teacher. It is not identical with the phase of becoming a student at a teacher education faculty.
- *Research in the phase of teacher preparation* investigating development of the professiona0lity of a teacher during their university preparation and what threatens it. Logically, its respondents are students studying in TE programmes.
- *Research in the phase of novice teachers* adapting to their new profession (usually up to the age of 30). This phase is most often omitted by researchers.
- *Research in the phase of a teacher being an expert* in his/her teaching profession, investigating threatening factors in teaching profession, level of feminization, gender differences, burn-out syndrome (often teachers older than 30).

Another way to view the scope of individual pedeutological research studies is according to the main categories of research themes/topics. As suggested by Kasáčová (2002), the most common areas of pedeutological investigations are:

- Teachers' attitudes;
- Relations between teachers and students;
- Requirements for teacher competence;
- Comparative study of teacher preparation in various countries;
- Evaluation of teachers' work;
- History of the teaching profession;
- Psychological study of teachers' personalities;
- Professiography of the teaching profession – teachers' professional activities.

It seems that the last one mentioned on this list, *professiography*, scientific research of the reality of the professional profession, is one of the most neglected key areas of research (Kasáčová, 2010, pp. 5–15). By *professiography*, we mean job-analysis or work description. These can be used as a research method dealing with systematic acquisition, description, analysis and evaluation of professional activities in the context of various assumptions for performance in one's profession (Kasáčová & Tabačáková, 2011, pp. 68–81).

The role of *professiography* is to find out about the specific activities of teachers during their everyday performance in the teaching position. It enables us to construct an image of this profession in each country. We decided to pay extra attention to this area of research in both periods studied in this book. The final product of pedeutological *professiography* is a *professiogram* – a description of the whole scope of daily, weekly and yearly professional activities of teachers in the context of their regular biodromal rhythm.

Although there was extensive research aimed at various aspects of teacher education, only a few thorough studies dared to investigate and reflect on the individual activities that constituted the performance of teachers. Thus, professiography started to be used more widely in various professions in the 1990s, after the fall of the restrictions of freedom of pedeutological research. Unfortunately, pre-primary teachers were lacking in it and the primary teachers were involved only marginally.

All of the-above mentioned research themes require adequate **research methods**. Chapter 2 provides an overview of research methodology primarily used before 1989 and examples of methodology being used after that year. Pedeutological research is social science research on human beings – teachers – and phenomena connected with their personality, relations and activities. That means that besides quantitative statistical methodology that many believe guarantees research objectivity, reliability and validity, qualitative research methods and their soft data should also be taken into serious consideration. All these points are observed and briefly mentioned in the overviews in both pre- and post-1989 periods. As the main frame of research methodology, reference publications by Slovak authors were used (Š. Švec, 2000; Gavora, 1996 & 2010).

1.2.3 Parallel research across countries/regions

The third approach complementing the above-mentioned diachronic view of pedeutological research in Central Europe is a kind of descriptive *comparative* approach, permitting the view of research on teachers *synchronically* across several countries.

Though the publication focuses on the history of research on teachers primarily in Slovakia, due to the historical coexistence with the Czech Republic for several decades, several chapters also share some information on the Czech research. Besides these two post-communist countries, other examples are also mentioned (Polish, East German, or Hungarian research), and many general characteristics might be considered as typical for the whole European post-communist region. Comparison is only lightly indicated, not addressed systematically, and the same applies to several comments on comparison of research in the Central European post-communist region with previously Western Block countries.

The data on educational research in Western countries come from several editions of the *American Educational Research Association's Handbook Series* (1963, 1973, 1986 & 2001) published by AERA (American Education Research Association) as well as from other resources, summarized by Hanesová (2009 & 2011).

Information from AREA handbooks serves as a wider context for comparison in this publication. Though these handbooks focus on general educational research, they include information on pedeutological research too. The first edition of the *AERA Handbook* (Gagé, 1963) described the educational research in the 1950's and at the beginning of 1960's, noting that it focused on *educational research in the Western countries*, specifically investigating the approaches to teaching the whole range of subjects at various grade levels which continued to be a crucial research topic throughout the whole following period. The second edition of the *AREA Handbook* (Travers, 1973), included information about research at the end of the 1960's and the beginning of the 1970's and showed that researchers started to pay more attention to pupils (their age, gender, cultural background – the factors/differences between pupils, etc.), their motivation or cultural deprivation. The third *AERA Handbook* presents educational research in the 1970's and the first half of the 1980's and it involved research into more sensitive issues of education (Wittrock, 1986).

Characteristics of pedeutological research studies carried out during the end of the 20th century and in the first decade of the 21st century were summarized in the fourth edition of the *AREA Handbook* (2001) as well as in the *International Handbook of Research on Teachers and Teaching* published, edited in 2009.

An overview of specific pedeutological investigations is presented in an extensive bibliography by Hanesová, which covers pedeutological research projects focused on the issue of professionalization of the teaching profession, teachers' competencies, the performance of the teaching profession in practice, working time, work load, contentment with the role of the teacher, the effectiveness of teaching, etc., in various countries (2009, pp. 219 – 250).

But, again, pedeutological research is an area that could be a subject of in-depth comparative investigation, and this publication should be considered as only a partial indication of this comparison via a few data.

2

Research on teachers before the year 1989

2.1 Historical context of educational research

As we mentioned already in the Introduction, the typical feature of teacher education and teacher research in Central Europe between 1948 and 1989 was the central control of the state over both, specifically that the Communist Party indoctrinated teachers and students with monistic Marxist-Leninist ideology and prohibited plural approaches and autonomy in the choice of values.

Political control of research meant ideological restrictions, prohibitions on certain topics, or sometimes even preventing certain types of research and prohibiting the use of certain research methods. Socialist education science was defined as political science (East German author König, 1967). Researchers were prohibited from citing some resources and, vice versa, were required to cite other sources (Gavora, 2004). But there are also examples that some authors avoided to fulfil the political expectations of the editors of journals on education and 'apolitical' studies, which were accepted for publishing. For instance, a scientific journal, *Pedagogika*, published a research study by Hrabal (1956), and commented positively on his initiative while disagreeing with his method of testing and some of his conclusions. Some authors were banned from publishing their documents, so they created and disseminated various 'samizdat' materials 'for internal use'. Some of them had to wait 20 years, until 1989, to be published (e.g. Maňák's book on Home Assignments at Primary School (1992), based on serious repeated research).

On the other hand, it would be wrong to consider the pedeutological research in Central and Eastern Europe as non-existent in the time of socialism. It has its own history in each individual country.

It is possible to start as early in the pre-WWII period with research completed by Chlup, a Czech educationist. In the 1930s, he formed his own experimental classroom where he tested the correctness of his own opinions on teaching grammar before he would ever teach it to his students who were future teachers (in Vaněk, 1967). Three research studies on teachers' careers were written by Vaněk in 1947. The interest in evaluation and educational research by Chlup and others stopped growing after the communist takeover in 1948. A Bulgarian comparative educationalist, Popov, describes this period as the darkest years for Bulgaria (2007, p. 271).

Educational research in political isolation behind the Iron Curtain logically prevented international contacts outside of the Socialist Bloc. Thus, comparative research studies on teachers were very limited and focused only on the countries within the Eastern Bloc. Researchers were expected to add some political statements into their research reports, e.g. praising the Soviet pattern for the Czechoslovak school reform or the 'excellent' publications written by Soviet authors (Omelka, 1955).

During a short reform period of building 'socialism with a human face' in Czechoslovakia in the 1960s, several leading members of a professional comparative education society publically criticized the prevailing ideology (Walterová, 2007, p. 261). For example, Skalková criticized the low level of educational research, included the one-sided deduction and empiricism, the cult of personalities and isolation, and restricted censorship (1963). The challenge was not only to build socialist humanism, but also a communist school in a true sense. Socialistic education, drawing on Comenius, was expected to represent the climax of our humanistic tradition (Loukotka, 1966). The challenge was to stop dividing educational science from Marxist ideology. The challenge was to shift from formal declarations to accepting Marxism as the real ground and method of education (Váňa, 1960). This period ended very soon after the Soviet military's suppression of the ideals of the Prague Spring in 1968 and soon after, the 'normalization' period started.

In 1973, the 14th Congress of the Czechoslovak Communist Party published a political document marking the issue of preparation for the teaching profession as an open problem on the state level. A collection of studies called *Studies on Teacher Education 1975* outlined the then-current tendencies in teacher education. It consisted of studies on school systems, contents of pre-service and in-service teacher education (for kindergartens, primary and secondary schools, as well as continuous education) in socialist Czechoslovakia, Bulgaria, Yugoslavia, Hungary, East Germany, Poland, Romania and the Soviet Union itself. All these studies dealt with similar problems in teacher preparation, especially with the need to guarantee the balance among three basic components of teacher education: a) ideological and political preparation (Marxism–Leninism); b) pedagogical (and psychological) preparation; and c) the specialized subject matter preparation (for the contents of the school subject). A study from Bulgaria marginally mentioned the necessity of research of university teacher trainers as well as the cooperation between universities and research institutions.

The *period of normalization* (1975–1986) in Czechoslovakia brought with it the return of censorship of all progressive ideas, inhibiting some authors from publish their books for ideological reasons (e.g. Maňák's publication on the issue of home assignments on his research in 1972, which was then published after the revolution in 1992). Most of their stories are not well-known because prohibition was never official, but only internal. In the beginning of this censorship era, several courageous civilians offered the banned authors the opportunity to publish under their names. But due to their rising fear of disclosure, these activities had only a short duration. In spite of this atmosphere, there had been many valuable studies written in this period. Democratically thinking authors who wanted to publish their scientific ideas decided to avoid ideological issues and deal with neutral topics and empirical research (Maňák, 2013, p. 389).

In 1975, the Czechoslovak state plan of scientific research was represented via a study published in a proceedings called *Pedagogical Sociology in Teacher Education* (Špendla, 1975). Its author criticized the lack of balance between an emphasis on teaching methodology and an emphasis on formative influence of teacher's work. Among other things, the research presented the points of conflict between the ideological upbringing in families and communist worldview formation in schools. Researchers used three different questionnaires to find out which two were related to teachers, to their influence in the process of worldview formation of pupils; and to the interaction between family and school, sadly viewing at it only from the side of teachers.

In 1975, Klímová compared social origin and the motives for becoming a teacher. It was the most extensive and detailed research on students at all faculties of education in the Czech Republic. The complex study *Učitel a jeho povolání*, written by a Czech author Pařízek (1988), used empirical findings of determinants and preconditions of the teaching profession. It was published after *Perestrojka* created an open path for information about the state of society and education (principle of 'glasnost').

The research on teachers in the second half of the 1980s showed signs of opening itself to the changes in society. The research came closer to the reality in schools; for instance, Průcha investigated teachers' real use of textbooks in the lessons and their communication with pupils (1985). Educational researchers expressed their criticism of the societal system more explicitly. It was evident, for example in the *Proceedings from the 10th Congress of the World Association for Educational Research,* which took place before the Velvet revolution from August 28th to September 1st, 1989 in Prague (though published shortly after the revolution in 1990).

In several of the studies of these *Proceedings,* the influence of 'Perestrojka' and indications of future political changes can be clearly recognized. *Macek* comments on the feasibility of establishing efficiency in education. He writes: "It is obvious that if pedagogy is to prove that the efficiency of education has increased, it is necessary to pass from proclamations and postulates to progressive forms of verification of the pedagogical reality, which would enable to find reasons for interventions bringing demonstrable results... Pedagogy must form a program of a conception of the pedagogical experiment as a subject of experimental pedagogy..." (pp. 802–805). In addition, *Skalková* underlined the need of critical approaches to education (p. 162). She emphasized the experiments carried out in education in other countries as well as the need of critical re-evaluation of the 'antique' in education, which opens doors to real innovations: "Czechoslovak school works in a dynamic, and at the same time very complicated period.... of profound changes in the economic, social and political spheres... Empirical researches concerning the real state of the practice have been developed, among others also in the frame of the basic research realized by the workers of the J. A. Comenius Institute of Education ČSAV.... Various aspect of education... have been submitted to a scientific analysis." (Skalková, 1990, p. 162). *Obdržálek* reflected on the purposes of a research of the educational system management in Czechoslovakia: "Pedagogical science has lagged behind the demanding objectives which call for a closer investigation. The reasons for this state of things are to be sought in its theoretical and methodological levels, in the need for a more complex and systemic analysis of education management..." (p. 452).

Also in these *Proceedings,* an evaluation of pedeutological research in socialist countries was described by Blížkovský (1990). According to him, it was focusing predominantly on teachers' education and the problems associated with the teaching profession, pointing to the balance of cognitive requirements for this profession, of teachers' skills, activities and abilities, and of teachers' personal character and value systems. "Pedeutological research in the European socialist countries is characterized especially by a growing integrating tendency seeking comprehensive correlative answers to questions of gnoseologically, praxeologically and axeologically orientated streams: what should be the minimum theoretical body of knowledge, practical expertise, abilities and qualities and what the person professionally involved in education should be like." Blížkovský himself carried out several professiographic studies of selected groups of educational employees (e.g. headmasters).

Although in the 1980s more attempts were undertaken to publically express one's criticism of educational research (e.g. Kulič, 1980; Byčkovský, 1983; Průcha, 1985), the only complex study presenting empirical research findings about the actual determinants and preconditions of the teaching profession was completed by Pařízek in 1988.

2.2 A general characteristics of research in education before 1989

Before 1989, education research tended to be politically biased in its aims and objects of study. The Czech comparative educationalist Walterová characterized the research prevalent in the then Czechoslovakia as a "one-sided 'criticism of bourgeois education' and (an) overestimation of Soviet education" (2008, p. 43, also Borevskaya, 2007 on the Soviet Union; Holik, 2008 on Hungary; Waterkamp, 2007 on East Germany – according to Manzon, 2011, p. 47–48). Moreover, the study of Western education systems was considered 'a potentially criminal act' (Popov, 2007; Walterová, 2007 – in Manzon, 2011, p. 48, 146). There were various obvious and hidden political reasons to avoid research topics that might reveal to any weaknesses in education. All the effort was invested into researching and publishing only positive results of socialist education.

Generally, an epistemological unification under the ideological umbrella of Marxism-Leninism "did not permit the development of objective and methodologically transparent comparative research" (Walterová,

2007, p. 257 – in Manzon, 2011, p. 146), nor any other thorough investigations on the teaching profession.

Based on the evaluation of a Czech educational expert Průcha, pedeutological research in socialist Czechoslovakia developed insufficiently in comparison with other countries and also in comparison with other areas of educational research (2002, p. 173, V. Švec, 2000). In spite of some attempts (e.g. Vorlíček, 1979; Kulič, 1980; Byčkovský, 1983; Průcha 1985), critical evaluation of TE empirical research was very rare before 1990 (Průcha, 2002, p. 173). Researchers in the Eastern Block had very limited access to Western scientific publications. Besides native authors, scientific libraries consisted of books in Russian, and some in the German language, publications in English were very rare in their collections even during the 1990s. Due to this fact, most educational researchers were insufficiently informed about research developments in other than Warsaw pact countries. The situation was not identical in all Eastern Bloc countries. E.g. Polish publications from the same period prove that their authors, Polish educators, were able to protect their freedom of access to French or American scientific publications (according to Maňák's post-communist reflection on the era before 1989, 2013).

However, according to Beňo, before 1989, a number of professional analyses and scientific research projects not dictated by ideological criteria were completed (2002, p. 173). Czechoslovak pedagogy and educational psychology were not uninformed or totally separated from educational trends in Western countries. Several authors and editors did their best to assist educational science to grow and develop, based on information from Eastern, but also Western countries. There are translations of some progressive books and reviews on some Western resources in recognized journals (for example, information on the *American Journal of Educational Research* in *Pedagogika*, 1957, No. 2; information about Freinet's experiment and educational problems in France, about a crisis in education in Western countries and about education in Israel, also on materials prepared by UNESCO in *Pedagogika*, 1958, No. 5 or 1965,

No. 6; information about the audio-visuals abroad – Mareš, 1976, No. 4.). For instance, in 1964, the journal *Pedagogika* published articles and reviews on the French and Italian education system, teaching non-Slavic languages, and group work in Western education/American schools. Gagne's *Conditions of Teaching* (1975) was published, although it presented behaviorism, which was generally sharply criticized by the official Marxist pedagogy and psychology (Průcha, 2002, p. 327). In cases where researchers got familiar with Western ideas, they might have proposed some progressive ideas, experimented with them and incorporated them into their theories, but their results were mostly ignored and their application controlled. In such cases, the researchers were often exposed to suspicion of collaboration with the 'enemies' of the state.

Regarding domestic research issues, they also were not adequately covered. According to Š. Švec (2000), none of the school reforms during socialism was based on a serious research and evaluation of the educational results. The most frequently applied ways of research were trial and error, common sense, personal experience and a method that relied on authority. The authority was represented by, first, the Central Committee of the Communist Party but also by influential politicians who often pretended to be scientists (Š. Švec, 2000, p. 9).

2.3 Institutional research before 1989

Before 1989, research studies on teachers were completed by researchers who were employees of educational institutes and universities or of research institutions and academies of sciences.

Some traces of institutional research on educational topics can be found before WWII, such as at the School of Higher Educational Studies in Prague and in Brno in the Czech Republic (since 1921). In Slovakia, two teaching academies in Bratislava and Prešov came into existence in 1931. In 1945, due to the Decree of the President of Czechoslovakia, No. 132/1945, the university level of the teaching profession was legislatively approved for teachers at all educational levels. This official university platform for research on teachers came into practice in 1946 after Act No. 100, when the existence of Faculties of teacher preparation at universities came into force. Thus, a serious opportunity for future development of progressive educational research arose at those institutions.

Very soon after the communist take-over in Czechoslovakia in 1948, the situation changed radically. In 1950, secondary level schools for pre-primary and primary teachers preparation, so called 'gymnasiums' (now grammar schools) substituted for faculties of education. The faculties of education continued to prepare teachers of secondary education. One explanation for this step was the rising demand for teachers due to the after-war boom in the birth rate. In the 1950s, the ministry of education established so-called 'research elementary schools' where educational researchers could have carried on their research experiments (especially for the purpose of solving problems related to teaching, and to writing textbooks (Chlup, 1956). Later on in 1959, these were substituted by the so-called pedagogical institutes of teacher preparation. Finally, in 1964, the status of the Faculties of teacher education came back to existence (Uhlířová, 2011).

Teacher-researchers from these tertiary institutions often carried out their research in cooperation with other universities from Warsaw Pact countries. For instance, in the years 1970–1975, the Faculty of education in Brno cooperated with tertiary level institutions of teacher education in East Germany (Dresden, Greifswald and Magdeburg), Poland (Poznan, Vratislav and Krakow), Hungary, and the Soviet Union (Voronez and Kiev). They focused on modern teaching aids, ideological problems of communist education in socialist schools, the new concept of education and preparation of primary teachers, the level of new normalized teacher preparation, and on parents' relationships with schools. Before the period of normalization, there were a few exceptions when educationalists from the Western countries got together with the

Eastern researchers (e.g. participants from the Netherlands, England, West Germany, Belgium in a pre-conference on Comenius in 1957 (Chlup, 1957).

Aside from universities and other institutions of tertiary education, educational research was carried out by several research centers. The Research Institute for Education in Prague, founded in 1945, was one of the first research centers in Czechoslovakia. Its role was to design school curricula and textbooks, and to focus on research. In the same year in 1945, it merged with another Research Centre in the Moravian metropolis of Brno and together they formed an Educational Research Institute named after J. A. Comenius, which was based in Prague. In 1946, there was a focus on assessing the physical state of school buildings in the Czech Republic and Moravia. Though this institution planned to carry out objective research, during 1948–1989, its research was strongly influenced by Marxist ideology.

In 1947/48, a Slovak version of the Research Institute of Education and the Pedagogical Institute in Bratislava, the capital of the Slovak part of Czechoslovakia, was founded. After the reorganization of the school system, the Slovak Academy of Sciences with its research centers played an important role as an agent of scientific research. Its cooperation with other socialist research institutions was significant (e.g. with the Academy of Educational Sciences in Moscow).

2.4 Foci of research on teachers before 1989

One of the first classifications of pedeutological research in Czechoslovakia before 1989 was produced by a Czech Vorlíček in 1984. The four categories in this classification reflected the facts about the ongoing research in education:

- Research into the characteristics of ideal teachers;
- Typology of teachers – e.g. Fišer (1966–1967);

- Opinions of pupils about teachers – e.g. Čulík (1973);
- Analysis of teachers' autobiographic memoirs.

In his overview of educational psychological research studies published in the Czechoslovak journal *Pedagogika* during 1951–1989, Mareš (2000) characterized the period between 1951 and 1968 as a period when the main emphasis of research was on the psychological processes of learning, then on pupils. Almost none of the research was on teachers. The next period, which was the period between 1969 to 1989 (especially the 1980s), was a period of research on communication and the interaction between teachers and students. This involved such a massive expansion of research that it was necessary to start to publish an extra series of collections of studies just so all the authors could have their reports (Průcha, 2000, p. 365). In this period, an interesting attempt to construct a typology of teachers took place (Hrabal & Lukš, 1971).

For example, research focused on the specifics of physics teaching and teachers was carried out by Ferko from Slovakia (1986). He observed 85 physics lessons for 7 to 9 graders and evaluated the effectiveness of instruction according to the active use of working time. He found that effectiveness of teaching differed significantly between the lessons of individual teachers.

A more complex view of the teaching profession in the context of the whole educational system was presented in the work of a Czech researcher Blížkovský (research mentioned in his publications 1967 and 1980). The censors forbid publication of the book *Hledání výchovné soustavy* (*The Search for the Educational System*) that he had prepared in 1968.

The following four Charts 1–4 present the same list of pedeutological research studies in pre-1989 Czechoslovakia, sorted chronologically as well as according to categories mentioned in the two classifications above (Chapter 1.2). Some parts of these charts have been published in several Proceedings in Slovakia recently (Hanesová, 2014, 2015).

Chart 1: Chronology of pedeutological research in Czechoslovakia (1948–1989)

Researched Areas	Researcher/Year of Publishing the Research
Teacher's career development	Vaněk (1947)
Activities of a form teacher (action research)	Omelka (1955)
Influence of teacher's activities on the discipline of students	Cipro (1955)
Teacher's teaching experience and teaching methods (action research)	Hrabal (1956)
Influence of an educational plan of a form teacher	Blížkovský (1959)
Pupils' opinions of teachers	Kurfürst (1962), Čulík (1973), Štefanovič (1967, 1974)
The influence of teachers upon the mental development of pupils	Pavlovič (1941, 1964)
The typology of the teacher personality	Fišer (1966/67)
Teachers' workload, fatigue in teachers' work	Ďurič (1969)
Democratization at schools and the teaching profession	Blížkovský (1967/68, 1980)
Psychological research of teaching staff	Liška (1969, 1970)
Grading by teachers and favorite subjects	The Laboratory of Pedagogy VUOS at SES (1971)
Teachers in society	Beňová (1972)
Reflection on school practice	Václavík (1972)
Communication between teacher and pupils	Tollingerová (1972)
The opinions of teachers-in-training on the socialist teacher profile, teachers' professional activities	Baláž (1973)

Stress in the teaching profession, the influence of the family/school upon the development of students, professiogram	Špendla (1974)
Communication between teacher and pupils	Milan (1975)
Comparison of the social origin and motives to become teachers	Klímová (1975)
Interaction between teacher and pupils in a traditional form of frontal teaching	Mareš (1975)
The influence of teachers upon the popularity of school subjects, the characteristics of a popular teacher	Lukš, Pelikán (1979)
Professiography – professional activities	Januška (1979)
The criteria of teacher effectiveness and its measurement	Kulič (1980)
The measurement of teaching results	Býčkovský (1983)
The evaluation of pedagogical research	Průcha (1985)
The problems of novice teachers	Horák, Kalhous (1985)
Teacher's health	Provazník (1985)
Teachers' skills	Langová, Kodým (1986)
The development of primary education	Čara (1986)
Teachers' abilities	Šturma (1986)
Physics teachers and their professional activities	Ferko (1986)
Stress and neurosis in teachers	Langová, Kodým (1987)
The teaching professional activities	Kučerová (1987)
Assessing the success of the teacher's work	Kodým, Fitl (1987)
Determinants and requirements for the performance of the teaching profession	Pařízek (1988)
Communication between teachers and students	Gavora (1987), Průcha, Hrdina (1987), Hupková (1987)
The use of schoolbooks and other teaching aids in the teaching process	Průcha (1985, 1989)

Research on students at all faculties of education in the Czech Republic	Stave pro sociální výzkum mládeže, Charles University (1986)
A microanalysis of school lessons	Bártková (1981), Zelina, Furman (1986,1988)

Chart 2: Research of biodromal development of teachers in Czechoslovakia

The phase of development of teaching professional career		
Research/ author	Time of research	Focus of research
Vaněk	1947	Research on teacher career
Klímová	1975, 1986	Comparison of social origin, motives of becoming a teacher by Ústav pro sociální výzkum mládeže at Charles University – most extensive and most detailed research of students at all faculties of education in the Czech Republic
The phase of preparation for teaching profession:		
Kalhous, Horák	Since 1985	Research on problems of novice teachers (publ. 1996)
The phase of stabilization teachers and identification with teaching profession:		
Štefanovič, Beňová	1967, 1974 1972	Research on images of pupils about an ideal teacher

Chart 3: Classification of research according to the main research areas (Průcha, 2002, p. 173) in Czechoslovakia

Research/author	Time of research	Focus of research
Teacher's attitudes and opinions		
Baláž	1968–1973	Opinions of pre-graduate teachers about the profile of socialist teacher (Question: Is there any harmony between the objective demands of a communist state and the subjective view of the students? Results: growing positive attitude toward state political ideological orientation: in 1967 – 39%, in 1973 – 42%)
Opinions of pupils/students on teachers		
Kurfűrst	1962	Opinions of pupils on teachers
Lukš, Pelikán et al (Educational Laboratory, Prague)	1971, 1973	Comparisons of favorite subjects with the characteristics of teachers, the issue of teacher's strictness in assessing the pupils, teacher's standard, the influence of pupil's diligence and talent on teacher's approach in lessons (via students' questionnaires, analysis, auto-diagnoses, assessment by school management)
Hrabal	1956, end of 1960ties, 1970-ties	Teacher's experience of teaching, teacher' image of the student, teacher's auto-diagnosing analysis based on the study results and secondary students' opinions about their subjects, their grades and their teacher.
Teacher's influence on children		
Pavlovič	1941, 1964	Influence of the teacher upon the mental development of children
Cipro	1952–1954	Observation of teacher's work – its influence on students
Communication between teacher and pupils		

Jurovský, Jurovská	1962	Research of interventions of educators in a care home for children
Tollingerová	1972	Teacher 79% – 12–15years old pupils 21%
Hrdina	1980s	Dialogue between teacher and pupils (open questions)
Průcha	1980s	Audio-recorded communication of teachers; complex analysis of instruction in primary school and in the grammar school via observation – activities of teachers and pupils, especially the time dimension, participation of pupils and the use of didactical means
Milan	1975	Interaction pupil – teacher
Mareš	1975, 1981, 1985	Interaction teacher – pupil, mostly during traditional form of frontal teaching
Hupková	1987	Communication teacher – pupil
Gavora (Institution of experimental Pedagogy of the Slovak Academy of Sciences	1987–1988	Communication during the instructional process in Slovak schools
Competencies of teachers		
Průcha	1985	Use of textbooks by teachers in the lessons
Langová, Kodým	1986	Teachers' skills
Čára	1986	Problems of primary schools and the contents of education, only partially on teachers (Question: recommendations how to improve the education in the primary schools, modifications of curricula, new textbooks, innovation of teaching methods);
Šturma	1986	Teachers' professional competencies
Evaluation of teachers' work		

Kodým, Fitl	1987	Evaluation of teachers' work by experts
Psychological characteristics of teacher's personality		
Ďurič	1969	Teachers' fatigue
Langová, Kodým	1986, 1987	Stress and neuroticism of teachers, their opinions on success and failure of pupils in a Prague primary school (Pygmalion effect). The authors also presented their research on the workload and mental disorders of Czech teachers in the 1980s, including the correlation between the successfulness of teachers and the structure of their mental state
History of teaching profession		
Cach, Schubert	1968 1987	Historic development of teaching profession – comparison of teacher education, social status, documents about the process of emancipation of teaching profession

In the year 2000, Průcha analyzed and summarized all research studies that took place between the years 1951 to 2000 in the educational journal, *Pedagogika*. Generally, the research before 1989 aimed predominantly at observing and analyzing the behavior of teachers, their communication with pupils, and their character and personality.

Professiography of a teachers' profession

Now a few words about research of professional activities of teachers in the pre-1989 period. Its beginnings can be traced back to the 1960s and 1970 (Jarešová, 2009; Babiaková &Tabačáková, 2009). Before 1989, professiography (job analysis) from a practical point of view was described as a method used for collecting data about certain professionals and their jobs (Bureš, 1981).

Chart 4: Examples of the use of professiography in research before 1989 in Czechoslovakia

Research/author	Time of research	Focus of research
Ďurič	1969	Research on teacher's activity (performance) in connection with fatigue – division from the point of view of societal expectations (a representative of society), psychology (in relation to pupils) as well as his/her own profession. According to his research in 1965/66 a 1966/67 the teaching load of 76% of teachers was 26 lessons and less; 32% of teachers spent over 30 hours in teaching and other professional activities (method: a questionnaire filled in by teachers and authorized by their headmasters)
Baláž	1972, 1973	1972: research of differences in the demands on teachers and the realities of teachers' lives, with over 1000 young teachers – to find out the effectiveness of the system of teacher preparation, research on the social conditions of young teachers, professional orientation, adaptation, further education, 1973: research on the professional activities of teachers, using the expression 'directing of teacher's activity'. In spite of the ideological background of this research, it is a valuable resource for examining the teaching profession in a historical perspective.
Špendla	1974 1975	Research using a psycho-professiogram, indicating signs of the ideology (e.g. scientific worldview, readiness to apply Marxism-Leninism in practice)

| Januška | 1979 | An attempt to create a professiogram of teachers' profession. It consisted of 6 basic levels of preconditions: physical, character, relations, methodological abilities, socio-political, and professional |
| Kučerová | 1987 | Research: professional activities of teachers |

Comparison with other countries

Prior to comparative research on teachers in post-communist countries, the main focus of general comparative educational research in communist countries was on the psychological process of learning, then on the analysis of the contents of school education in comparison with the situation in capitalist countries. This research was geared toward finding out students' favorite subjects. As Cipro informed us in 1967, this kind of research involved vast samples, e.g., 4000 pupils in East Germany. Gradually more and more attention was paid to the learners. But very little empirical research was focused on teachers.

In countries with a long tradition of empirical research on teaching as an occupation, professiographic research started already in the 1950s, e.g. in the USA (Becker 1953). Since the 1970s, the use of ethnographic methods meant to reveal real teachers' performance has been developed (Waller & Lortie 1969). Soon, it became evident that such professiographic studies had huge theoretical significance in understanding teachers' identities and work.

The development of research on teachers' professionalism and their professional activities in Western countries has been described in a very brief way by Troman (2007). According to his overview of research in the Annex to a short history of research on teaching professionalism, researchers in the Western countries started to focus on the concepts of 'professionalism' and 'professionalization' since the 1970s (see also Goodson & A. Hargreaves 1996) when two approaches to the study of teachers' roles, their identities and professionalism started to be evident:

- Interpretivist/interactionist perspectives on teachers' work and the social processes of schooling: Not only in the USA, but also in the UK the interpretive/interactionist studies focused on the empirical examination of teacher strategies (e.g. Woods 1979) and teacher/school cultures (e.g. Pollard 1985). There was a growing importance of ethnographic methodology for the study of teachers and teaching reflected in the publication of classics such as Ball (1981) and A. Hargreaves (1986);
- Neo-Marxist perspectives on professionalism, work and teachers' relations with the capitalist State (e.g. Ozga 1988) with an urgency of developing a sociology of teachers' work.

2.5 Research methods used in pedeutology before 1989

In the Eastern Bloc, the period between 1945 and 1989 was characterized with a) its predominantly quantitative research methodology; b) 'scientific' tendencies to guarantee objectivity and impartiality; and c) proclamations that the aim of research was to verify or testify existing theory. Due to the ideological situation, the researchers avoided openly interviewing teachers or parents about their opinions on various educational phenomena (Průcha, 2002).

Besides two basic categories of research methodology – predominantly quantitative and predominantly qualitative (Š. Švec et al, 1998) – another point of view was used for a new classification by Vorlíček (1979) in Czechoslovakia. He distinguished two categories of research methods according to the approach to the researched phenomena: a) direct methods (observation, experiment and analysis of products of activities); and indirect (mediated) methods (literary methods, study of documents, analysis of school experience).

Qualitative methodology already began to be mentioned in Czechoslovak studies in the 1960s. The journal, which was published in 1966, was a study about comparing the analyses of the use of quantitative and qualitative methods (Gončarov, No.2). In 1983, a Czech methodologist by the name of Skalková, listed the five most commonly used quantitative methods in Czechoslovak educational research. These include interviews, questionnaires, observation, experiments, and didactic tests (according to Galla & Sedlář, 1983, p. 119).

In the later decades of the period, qualitative methodology – for instance casuistic and case studies – gradually started to penetrate into educational sciences as an influence from other social sciences, such as sociology, ethnography, and psychology (e.g. Prague group of school ethnography in the former institution Ústav pedagogických a psychologických výskumů). As was the case during the communist era, these sciences had a much smaller impact on education than they did in developed countries. For instance, in the USA, qualitative methodology began to be widely applied than in those countries.

An interesting example of how qualitative methodology was gradually finding its place in educational research in Czechoslovakia was described by Václavík as early as 1972. These years were typical with their tendency to criticize the insufficient connection between theory and educational practice. One of the ways of dealing with this was the suggestion that professional teachers should do their own research in their own classrooms. To connect theory to practice, so called 'pedagogical/ educational reading' began to be used in 1956 Auerswald, 1956). It started with writing reports for parents and continuing by teachers reading their observations from their teaching practice to the professional public. The reports were descriptions of individual experience, very seldom with any theoretical explanation or generalization of experience for better understanding of the educational problems of schools. Then the value of these writings was evaluated according to the level of a professional way of responding to educational and psychological issues, but these criteria were not strictly fixed. It was often too subjective, too superficial, too empirical, and too practical (very little theory). They used to emphasize the theory but did not include a sufficient number of experiments. Still, the organizers of this pedagogical teaching achieved one thing: they avoided the biggest deformation of the 1950s, the overall generalization of educational principles.

Their first aim of these 'readings' was to stimulate teachers to study pedagogy and psychology, and to bring into harmony scientific research and practice. Later on, they were required to analyze their experiences, to evaluate and classify the factors and to write conclusions. The teachers' teaching journal reading became a real prompt for several researchers as well as ordinary teachers of primary and secondary schools to begin conducted documented research. During the first decade, the 1950s, there was 1236 Czech and 325 Slovak studies written for this purpose, which were read on various levels (district, central), and heard by about 2000 listeners per year. The best research was published.

It appears that in the 1950s and 1960s, the interest of individual teachers in the subject matter and the core school subjects was higher than was interest in research work and in ideological and political formation. Research also focused on the contents of individual subjects, which was in accord with the trend of Western research studies and the contents of various school subjects and their teaching (Maňák, 2004).

According to several research reports and theoretical studies on educational research methodology published during the communist era, the following educational research methods were used in research on teachers between 1960 and 1989:

- Micro research and teacher's diaries – teacher's self-reflection of one's own activities, their evaluation by the teacher, students, parents (1955, 1956, 1962);
- Observations of pedagogical communication and interaction during lessons with verbatim minutes from audio-recorded observed lessons (1955, 1962, 1971, 1975, 1979, 1981, 1985, 1986, 1988, 1989);
- Interviews (1955, 1979);
- Studies of educational documents (1959, 1979);

- Historical analysis (1962);
- Historical ethnography of education – study of oral history (1971);
- Logical analysis (1962);
- Experiments (1962, 1968, 1978, 1979, 1980, 1983, 1986);
- Pedagogical statistics (1968);
- Comparative studies (1968);
- Theoretical analysis (1968);
- Questionnaires (1972, 1979, 1985, 1987, etc.);
- Didactic tests (1979);
- Sociometric methods (1979);
- Analyses of products or activities (1979);
- Analyses of school experience (1979);
- Focus groups (1979);
- Casuistry (1977, 1966); case studies (1983);
- Prognostic methods (1979, 1980, 1987).

Comparison with research foci and methods in other/ Western countries

After presenting the categories and methods of research on teachers in the Eastern Bloc, let us briefly compare them with research in the Western Bloc.

The tendency to prefer direct, quantitative research, especially experiments, in the first two decades after WWII could be likened to the situation in Western countries. LeCompte (2009) characterizes the first edition of *AERA Handbook on Educational Research* (Vol. N. L. Gage, 1963), describing **the 1950s and the early 1960s**, as an expression of "disdain for non-experimental research" (p. 35). It showed that experiments and quasi-experiments, measuring classroom behavior by systematic observation, the use of statistics and rating methods, testing cognitive skills and achievement, and measuring non-cognitive variables in research on teaching were the typical features of research in the Western world as well.

In *the 1960s and beginning of the 1970s,* the researchers started to reflect various new issues connected with research, such as the subjectivity of the researcher, asymmetry of power or the need for a collaborative effort. The most common object of educational research was not teachers, but pupils. Though researchers in Western countries became more and more aware of various problems and pitfalls of qualitative research, the second edition of the AERA Handbook (Vol. R. M. W. Travers, 1973) indicated that non-experimental research design started to emerge. The move toward a more critical epistemological approach was evident. In the research methodology of this decade, a shift toward direct observation of early childhood teaching; the assessment of teacher competence; instrumentation of research in teaching; the analysis of qualitative data; and pitfalls in research (mainly with regard to experiments) took place. In Czechoslovakia, educational researchers in this period typically used didactic tests, interviews and simple statistical methods of data processing.

The next decade of *the 1970's and the first half of the 1980's* witnessed intensified discussion of the following thematic issues (the third edition of the *AERA Handbook* (Vol. M. C. Wittrock, 1986): theory and methods of research on incorporating research into teaching and the teacher; the social and institutional context of teaching; research on the teaching of subjects and grade levels; paradigms and research programmes; the philosophy of research on teaching; measurement of teaching; quantitative and qualitative methods in research on teaching; observation as inquiry and method; and the synthesis of research on teaching. This third edition reflected the move from a focus on objective research to more 'inspirational', though more subjective, scientific research. "Interpretivism, phenomenology, critical and post-modern theory, symbolic interactionism and constructivism provided alternatives to behaviorism and functionalism" (LeCompte, 1986, pp. 3–42). Besides researching macro-processes by means of questionnaires, tests and observation sheets, researchers focused more on micro processes using more elaborate observation methods, video recording, diaries, ethnographic interviews and action research received legitimate positions among research methods. A collaborative form of research was highly recommended.

In Czechoslovakia, researchers in this period started to use more questionnaires. Simple observation was increasingly replaced by interactional analysis and audio recordings (Mareš, 2000). In the period between 1969–1989, researchers typically created many psycho-diagnostic tests. Simple statistics were replaced by classical descriptive statistics (Mareš, 2000).

Comparing the data from research studies in Czechoslovakia with data in the three editions of AERA Handbooks on research in the Western countries, it is possible to see that researchers in Czechoslovakia used similar research methods. Though some of them emerged a little bit later and the ratio between quantitative and qualitative methods had different values, the above-presented overviews seem to bring enough evidence to say that, very generally, the educational and pedeutological research methodology in Czechoslovakia developed in similar developmental stages as research in the Western countries.

3

Pedeutological research after the year 1989

To comprehend the changes in the paradigm of pedeutological research after the democratic revolution of 1989, it is necessary to understand its wider societal and educational context. For this reason, chapter 3.1 is rather detailed, sharing the components of the transformations that took place in post-communist countries. Following these details, the question about the changes in pedeutological research in a post-communist country will be investigated.

This chapter focuses primarily on the **first phase of the transition period (1990–2005)** that to took place right after the democratic revolutions in 1989. In 2004, most post-communist countries joined EU and their access to research opportunities widened radically. The fact of integration into the OECD and EU set new, higher demands on the building of a knowledge-based economy and society. Romanian and Hungarian authors (Birzea, 1996; Halász, 2007 – according to Kosová & Porubský, 2011) called this new period the 'second transition' of the educational systems. Thus, **the second (present) phase** of reforms (2005 – nowadays) involves reconstruction efforts related to professional standards for teachers, creating conditions for professional development of teachers, changes of the system of teacher preparation, of the status of teachers and their professional identity.

Being given vast opportunities for international exchanges and EU research grants, etc., as well as the boom in information technologies and internet access, the amount of research taking place in the former European socialist countries has grown radically. That is why the post-2004 studies mentioned in this publication are chosen with no intention of countrywide coverage or inter-regional comparison, but simply to provide examples of main topics within pedeutological research methodology.

3.1 Historical context – transformation of education system since 1989

After the democratic revolutions in Central and Eastern Europe in 1989, its citizens had to face a fast and turbulent period of changes, especially due to rapid rotation among ruling political parties. They could not have been adequately prepared for this sudden release of state control. The rather inexperienced politicians were under pressure to prepare new legislation aimed at building parliamentary plural democracy at different levels of local government, allowing participation of various political parties and civic institutions in the government. Besides that, economic reconstruction and privatization, and particularly education aiming to teach people how to make wise use of their new freedom and personal responsibility were certainly among the biggest challenges of the transition period.

The process of transformation in education in post-communist countries followed the political and societal events in the country. It was described e.g. by Kosová & Porubský (2011, pp. 26–27) as involving the following four phases:

- **Deconstruction** demonstrated in negation of the previous state after the revolution in 1989 (with its abolition of the leading role of the Communist Party and acceptance of basic rights of citizens);
- **Stabilization,** gradual reconstruction and modernization of education systems, demonstrated in analyzing the previous state and discussions about it, creating new legislation, first ideas of a systematic educational reform, educational innovations and experiments;

- **Complex reconstruction of the educational system,** which included adoption of national educational curricula; and
- **Implementation and (relative) stabilization,** implementation of change into school practice.

As Kosová & Porubský (2011) observed, though the last phase is typical for most post-socialist countries, several doubts and various complicated political issues associated with reform resulted in new destabilizing processes. Some transforming countries, including Slovakia, have been under the pressure from two determining and dilemmatic perspectives. The historic perspective had a dilemma of what to leave and what to retain in the existing system. On the other hand, the developmental perspective faces the dilemma of where to aim during the process of integration into the globalized world represented by the Western democracies. According to Kosová & Porubský and experts they refer to (p. 25), the bottom-up way of transformation of the school system in post-socialist countries was not feasible in the first years of their democratic development. Implementation of innovations might be successful only after reaching a very high, "excellent level of provision of basic legislative, organizational, financial and personal conditions for de-centralization, evaluated self-managements of schools, and especially for the quality and sufficient number of educational professionals and their professional development" (p. 25).

The transformation of education supported by strong pro-Soviet ideology has been a demanding and often very painful process. The socialist education system had a respectable, but unrealistic aim: to provide 'versatile' education for all young people (Velikanič, 1978, pp. 35–41)[1] including a good balance of all kinds of skills with a high command of updated scientific and technological knowledge,

---

[1] defined in the documents of the Communist Party, e.g. *About the close connection between school and life and about the further development of education in Czechoslovakia"* from 1959; implemented into the text of all compulsory study materials for university teacher preparation, e.g. in Velikanič's textbook for university students for the faculties of education in 1978.

physical fitness, and sense for collectiveness. Schools had to prepare young people for productive work, ability to contribute and defend the communist state, finding enjoyment and satisfaction in working for the whole community, and being filled with ideas of socialistic patriotism and internationalism.

Officially declared aims of 'harmonious, complex mental and physical development' of young people included the development of one's senses, strong will, good memory, pragmatic skills and habits, logical thinking, the ability to construct one's own opinions and convictions and critical comments. It also included appropriate motives, needs and habits; desirable emotional relations and attitudes; creative imagination and physical health. Such dimensions of personality development were to be pursued and implemented in a) ideological-political education, b) moral education, c) intellectual (cognitive) education, d) technological education, e) aesthetic education and f) physical education. The education system targeted at equipping the school graduates with practical skills, preparing them for active life in the society, for positive development of personal life in harmony with the general development of society. The requirement was even to teach children to solving current and future problems, using the historical knowledge and scientific generalization of historic experience.

These were excellent aims, but because in most cases the freedom of teachers' and pupils' to think creatively and critically was limited by the ideological and political restrictions, they could not be fully developed and in many cases they remained only verbal proclamations. The communist education system often relied on indoctrination combined with the overuse of 'Herbartianism', which is a schematized and normalized way of teaching and school work (Somr & Hrušková, 2014). It also relied on its very strict procedures, teachers imposing the new data on the pupils, focusing heavily on the cognitive side of learning, rigid inspections, and 'etatism' – an exaggerated emphasis on state interventions in education. A serious change in educational, as well as in research paradigms was needed.

Very soon after the political pressure dissolved, a **humanistic educational paradigm**, already well-established in Western educational systems – started to penetrate into the disputed area of education. After decades of underestimating individual teachers' and students' needs, humanization of education in the Czech and Slovak Republics (in accord with the educational aims of EU and OECD) was expected to fill in the following gaps:

- Need of moral revival of the humanity.
- Respect of children's rights.
- Criticism of traditional school from the position of a child (uniform education, non-existing individual approach, passivity of children, high level of directivity, small space for independence, creativity, activity, positive experience), the need to see the child as a child and active subject, not just as a pupil or an object of education.
- Democratization of school: All should have equal educational opportunities for development of their talents. Parents and children should become school partners.

Since the end of the communist regime in the 1990s, a number of radical steps have been introduced into the legislation of education in all post-communist countries. In Slovakia, the transformation of the last socialist Education Act (from 1984) consisted of 28 legislative reforms for all levels of schools between the years 1994 and 2000. The post-communist transformation required in particular:

- Abolition of aims and contents based on the ideology of the previous Communist era;
- Abolition of the principle of uniformed state school system and opening the legalized possibility to found private and church schools;
- Starting the process of humanization of education;
- Preparing better educational opportunities for pupils aged 14–18;

- Decentralization of management and delegation of power on districts and school boards.

The implementation of a humanistic approach to education that began in the 1990s was based on new emphases, such as promoting personal uniqueness and self-development as the aims and condition of education; holistic development of personality and priority of relationships in the life of a specific person, and the priority of attitudes and abilities (Kosová, 2000). The previous aim, to produce a harmoniously educated person in all areas of education, was changed into aiming for the complex development of a personality due to his/her own specific abilities.

The development of the teaching' profession was radically influenced by the changes in the philosophy of education during and after the period of the first transition reforms in Central and Eastern Europe education in the 1990s. In the context of the previous historic development, personalized and humanistic orientation of the teachers in a post-communist society was a big challenge. It expected teachers to become fully functional self-realized personalities with their own style of teaching. This emphasis went hand in hand with the cognitive/constructivist approach, preparing teachers as reflective professionals, or with the social re-constructivism model, which viewed teachers as the innovative agents of social change. With a fair amount of simplification, the 1990s can be described as a shift from teaching facts using indoctrinating, encyclopedic approaches to developing humanistic, constructive, reflective ways of teaching how to think.

The emphasis of **teacher education** was shifted to prepare new teachers who would be capable of teaching, in accordance with the principles of humanistic education, i.e. to

- Tolerate feelings, interests, needs and individual differences of each child, their learning styles, opinions, problems;
- Reflect on their own mistakes and weaknesses;

- Create welcoming environment enabling success of all children, curiosity, questions, discussion, open communication, stimulating ideas, criticism;
- Support independent thinking and activity; searching for different approaches, diversity of solutions, non-traditional solutions, positive relation of the child to learning, positive non-formal cooperative relationships between teacher and children, child's awareness of the need for self-improvement;
- Require active, conscious discipline and responsibility; child's ability to express their own opinions and of self-assessment; and reject blind obedience, enforced activity, atmosphere of fear and tension, mocking children, dividing children 'into boxes', satisfaction with the average achievement, unambiguous approach, lack of independence.

In the first decade after the revolution, the above-mentioned needs for change in education and teacher education were pronounced but there was not enough time and experience to put them into practice so that they would influence normal school life deeply enough. In 2002, Š. Švec, a Slovak research methodologist, noted that the science was still influenced by residue from the period of totalitarian indoctrination (p. 78).

That is why the *National Program of Education in the Slovak Republic for 10 – 15 years – Project Millennium (2000–2015)* was initiated. Its main focus was on the transition of approaches.

Chart 5: *Project Millennium* – suggested changes in education

FROM	TO
Passing on encyclopedic knowledge on the pupil	Holistic development of child's personality, including the ability how to learn
Passivity	Activity, independence, creativity
Uniformity, centralism	Variability, plurality

Authoritarianism, dogmatism	Humanization
Myth of an unerring teacher	Teacher – adviser
Focus on an average pupils	Differentiated and individualized approach
Frontal methods (with the whole class)	Group work
Competitive tasks	Cooperation of children
Focus on the content	Focus on the whole process (education)
Chalk, blackboards	ICT
Isolated subjects	Integrated teaching
Receptive and reproductive methodology	Heuristic methodology
Subjective examination of individual children in front of all other pupils	Objective forms of testing, self-assessment, positive evaluation
Homework	Ideas for free time activities
Focus on discipline and obedience	Focus on acceptance of pupils, respect
Dominance of teacher's word and textbooks	Authentic resources of information
Preference of verbal and mathematical-logical intelligences	Equality of all 8 intelligences (Gardner)
Development of the left brain hemisphere	Development of the both brain hemispheres
Predominantly intellectual	Balance between cognitive, affective, psycho-motoric
Fixed grouping (classes)	Natural grouping of pupils according to aims of education
Isolation of school from life	Connection with the life of community

In her analysis of the first decade of educational reform in Slovakia, Mikulová (2006), a representative from the Methodology and Pedagogy Centre (an institution for in-service teachers' education and training), also criticized several features of the transformation in education between 1993 and 2006, stating that in spite of the passage of 16 years since the political changes, there was no sign of a radical reform of the school system in Slovakia:

- All governments treated the education reform as a political matter (always wanting to start from zero). They issued new Acts but in-school practices were not substantially influenced by these Acts.
- All changes were impressed upon teachers mostly top-down – by centralized and administrative means, instead of 'bottom up' initiatives (which actually occurred in the 1990s but at that time the state policy did not support them).
- The state expressed willingness to deal with problems, but in a fragmented way, via government departments, not cross departments.
- Underestimation of the high degree of inertia and conservatism in the school system.
- Everything expressed as in visions (e.g.: the Millennium project) and political proclamations with no practical steps done by a professional management.
- Deficit of an overall profile of the teaching program graduates that would include a list of specific competencies.

In spite of this very ambitious program of humanization of the school system in post-communist countries, there were problems with its application. At about the beginning of the new Millennium, a few Czech (Walterová, 2002) and Slovak (Kosová, 2009) pedagogical experts spoke openly about the **crisis of teaching profession** in their countries (e.g. Walterová, 2001; Kosová, 2009). Inter alia, they point at feminization (ČR – over 80% women) and aging of teachers (ČR – 50 years old – average), or at the deficient qualifications of teachers on a national level, the decreasing attractiveness of this profession, the shortage of teachers as well as rising societal expectations of teachers. According to Kosová, in the year 2000 the teachers in this region were not sufficiently prepared to build a learning society based on knowledge (Kosová, 2005).

Awareness of this crisis raised several challenges. One of them was to enhance the status and quality of pre-graduate preparation of teachers and defining teachers' profiles while paying attention to the context of educational situations. Another was the significant need to raise the social status of teachers and to start considering them as autonomous subjects was explicitly formulated (Kosová, Pupala, 2004). Kasáčová & Kosová (2006), who are university teacher-education representatives, reason that in the history of Slovakia, teachers have always been engaged in the societal changes. During socialism, they were under a considerable ideological pressure, and after 1989, they were criticized for supporting the last regime, as if they had no backbone. In the beginning of the Millennium they were criticized that they were not able to solve the 'modern' problems of their pupils. They have been searching for their professional identity, for authentic professional autonomy, for the ability to generate the standards of performance and the ethical codes of the teaching profession. At the beginning of the Millennium, the efforts of teacher education started to focus more intensively on assisting teachers to define their competencies, their professional knowledge in action and the emphasis on self-reflection, to solve the tension between the pedagogical and specialist preparation of teachers (Kosová, 2006).

In Slovakia, the compulsory transition of teaching education from a non-structured to a structured model with two degrees (B.A and M.A) according to the Bologna Declaration, hindered the process of progressively developing the model of teacher education (Kosová & Tomengová, 2015, p. 40). Sadly enough, often these documents were prepared by staff 'sitting around the green table' without the continuous interaction with people who actually understand school practice. This top-down approach has been especially reflected in state legislation regarding how teachers should implement educational reforms in their teaching (Kosová & Porubský, 2011, pp. 17–27).

In order to start solving the crisis of the teaching profession via accentuating the professional standards for this profession, *The Competence Profile of the Pedagogical Employee* was elaborated by a team of educational experts in Slovakia in 2006. It consisted of three categories of teachers' key competencies that the teacher education faculties should prepare their graduates for (Kasáčová et al, 2006):

Competencies needed for communication with pupils:

- To identify the individual characteristics of the pupils: to get to know the pupil via an educational diagnosis and to be able to deal with the individual specifics of the pupil;
- To identify the psychological and social factors of the pupil's learning (teaching style);
- To identify the socio-cultural context of the pupil;

Competencies connected with the educational process:

- To mediate the educational content (to be familiar with the content of the school subject; to be able to plan and design the instruction, to set appropriate aims and objectives, to do the analysis of the state curriculum, to choose and implement appropriate methodology, to assess and evaluate the educational process);
- To create conditions for learning and education (positive climate, materials and technological background);
- To facilitate the personal development of pupils (to be able to influence it, to develop pupils' social skills and attitudes, to prevent and remedy socio-pathological phenomena and behavioral disorders;

Competence of teacher's self-development:

- To have the ability to initiate and direct their professional growth and self-development (self-diagnosis, self-reflection);
- To identify oneself with the professional role and with the school.

In spite of all the above-written efforts, *TALIS* – the international research study of the practice of teachers in lower secondary schools (2008) found out that during the 18 months before the study, up to 80% of participants tended to teach according to the traditional, transmission, teacher-centered way. Slovak teachers used significantly less independent and creative activities than the average TALIS countries. This finding was evidence of a need of yet another, really radical change in the education system.

In 2008, in Slovakia, the actual educational reform finally launched with several new educational regulations and laws that had been designed, such as the *Act on Education*, the Regulation for Pre-primary institutions – Kindergartens, and specifically, the State educational program. The *Act on 'Pedagogical' Employees* issued in 2009 categorized all school educational employees; it defined their rights, prerequisites and duties as well as the possibilities of career development). The *Act on Education* No. 245/2008 Z.z. (o výchove a vzdelávaní) in 2008 envisioned the following changes (Chart 6):

Chart 6: Suggested changes in education in *The Act on Education* No. 245/2008 Z.z.

FROM	TO
The school: gives children information prescribed by the state centralized curriculum	The school: gives children what has been agreed with the partners (users) (school curriculum)

The head-master: controls the activity of teachers	The head-master: cares so that the teachers would be able to give the best
Teachers: pass the ready-prepared knowledge (the only recognized truth) the pupils	Teachers: organize pupils' activity, cooperate with the pupils, facilitate in their learning process – process of acquiring knowledge and skills
Pupils: a passive attitude of accepting ready-prepared information from the teachers, solving typical homework assignments	Pupils: active, working in teams, solving project assignments, acquiring new knowledge and skills via problems solving
Parents: passively watch the activity of the school	Parents: cooperate in the process of school syllabus design, help/ participate in the school activities

Observations of the experiences of schools so far show that the long-awaited reform still has not brought much needed changes in education. The impact of the 2008-reform is currently being investigated (via research APVV No. 0713-12 *Implementation of Curricular Reform in Primary Schools in Slovakia* since 2015). Still, it is possible to say that the transformation in this region has been dependent on an intensive intervention of the state (Kosová & Porubský, 2011, p. 17). Thus, it is possible to say that this reform had predominantly a **top-down** direction. Such transformation has had a profound impact on the teaching profession (Hroncová, 2001; Korim, 2011).

These attempts at change should be compared with transformations in Western democratic countries, which typically involve a systematically-managed process of gradual change. A gradual, more systematic process of **bottom-up** changes in education is based primarily on the initiative of teachers in the school practice, and not so much on a state's intervening after ensuring basic democratic frameworks, effective innovation management and bottom-up systematic changes are feasible.

This has been the main deficit of educational reform in some post-communist countries.

3.2 Transformation of pedeutological research

Though right after the Fall of the Iron Curtain in 1989 the door to freedom of investigation was opened, its development in the beginning of 1990s was complicated and difficult for each of the former Eastern Bloc countries. Immediately after 1989, research in educational sciences was also minimized because of dampening the voice of faculties of education.

The main questions were: What are the consequences and impact of political changes going to be in teaching professions? Which changes were expected or proclaimed, and which are actually taking place in schools and in the teaching profession?

With regard to research institutions in Czechoslovakia, during the first three years several research institutions ceased to exist, e.g. the Research Institute of Education was dissolved or the Institute of Experimental Pedagogy – a department of the Slovak Academy of Sciences. Also, the Slovak Pedagogic Society fell apart in the early 90's, and although it resumed its activities in 2002, it did not regain its previous level of respect (Kosová, 2011, p. 24). In the Czech Republic, the Educational Institute JAK ČSAV was dissolved. But, in 1993, the Czech Association of Educational Research (ČAPF) came into existence, encouraging pedeutological research in the Czech Republic. Now, among the most active research institutions are the *Štátny pedagogický ústav – State Educational Institute, Ústav informácií a prognóz školstva – The Institute of Information and Prognoses of Education* (in Slovakia) and *Ústav výzkumu a rozvoje školství – The Institute of Research and Development of Education* (Czech Republic).

In 1991, Krejčí commented on vast discrepancies between the proclaimed state of education and its research; and the reality in schools. In order to give speedy assistance in such a situation, he suggested to researchers in the faculties of education start with 'micro' research studies. His critique was directed against the deformations that resulted from the unrealistic aim of the communist educational system – striving for the versatile development of a person. He pointed out that in fact it turned out to be a system of human deformation according to the rules of hostility (between the parties in the society). He also challenged the value system that remained from the communist regime (the communist moral codes) which used to be obligatory for all citizens of socialist countries and became embedded in people's everyday behavior. This included learning things by heart, just repeating what was prescribed without thinking about the content, and expressing one's own opinion. To change this was one of the most radical challenges in the area of scientific research in the new democracies. It was obvious that there was a need of not only an extrinsic, but also an intrinsic reform in education.

The following example of research on teachers shows the protracted character of this reform. During the first three years (1990–93), there was not enough time for a radical change. According to Havlínová's survey in the Czech Republic in 1993, about 95% teachers taught in the same ways as they had been taught under the socialist system. They seemed to show the same weaknesses: a passive approach to teaching, a low level of creativity and motivation, an absence of self-reflection, professional dependence on higher commands and non-professional behavior in many areas. According to the OECD estimation, in 1995 there were only about 15–20% reforming, innovative teachers in the Czech Republic with the remainder apparently not changing their ways of teaching (Spilková, 1997, p. 50).

In 1997, Spilková commented on the need of an analysis of the period right after the political changes in the first half of the 1990s in the Czech Republic: "There has not been done a serious analysis of the present or 'before-November' analysis of the Czech school." (p. 10).

According to Spilková, most of the analyses ignored the ideological deformations (though the most substantial of them were removed after 1990) and therefore generalizing about this area are very difficult. So far, an in-depth analysis was simply substituted with a general diagnosis of basic problems and needs, which was evident in the publications from that era – various studies in media, as well as partial probes by some teachers, headmasters, and students of teacher education.

Some attempts to carry out investigations of teachers in the first decade of the new era of Central European countries revealed important facts. E.g. Mintrop (1999) tried to determine the degree of the radical educational reform in the thinking and behavior of teachers in the previously East Germany. Using observation and interviews with teachers in eight schools, he found an imbalance between the theoretical proclamations of teachers and their behavior. Their behavior has not changed much and their approach to new methods could be described as 'waiting'. The respondents were satisfied with their previous education and their response to new initiatives was strongly marked by their former 'pedagogical' conviction, accepting only those new approaches that have some association with their previous experiences. This confirms the words of Bronfenbrenner, who wrote that "teaching behavior is influenced by the context in which it is situated" (1979). "Faculty members' teaching decisions depend on the interplay of individual beliefs and values, which have been shaped by their previous education and training, and the norms and values of the contexts in which they work." (Singer, Nielsen & Schweingruber, (eds.) 2012, p. 177).

A study among teachers in the Central-Slovak region showed that substantial changes in teachers' opinions and attitudes started to emerge in the second half of the 1990s. According to Kosová (1996, 1997), 50% of respondents in 1993 showed their adherence toward tradition and 50 % of respondents showed in favour of incoming change and innovation. In 1996, their number reduced to 40%. In 1993, only 15% of respondents implemented truly innovative, even systemic changes in their teaching, in 1996 this number grew to 25%.

A very important section of research on teachers was the investigations on the social status of teachers. Around 2000, some researchers (Rosa, Turek, Zelina, and other authors of *Project Millennium*) said that the overall situation of teachers in 2000 was worse than before November 1989. A comparison of two surveys in 1992 and 2000 (Kika, 2002) showed that the sense of dissatisfaction of teachers declined (e.g. due to the chronically low financial rewards).

Several surveys were completed on the perception of the working and social conditions and motivation for professional improvement (Beňo, 2001; Turek, 1999; Porubská, 1997; Valica, 2001).

On the other hand, the 1990s are characteristic with a boom of textbooks on research methodology, encouraging, among other things, research on teachers (Maršálová & Mišík, 1990; Kučera, 1992; Disman, 1993; Maňák et al., 1994; Průcha, 1995; Š. Švec et al, 1998; Turek, 1998; Hendl, 1999; Strauss & Corbinová, 1999; Ferjenčík, 2000; Gavora, 2001; Ritomský, 2002; Plichtová, 2002; Juszczyk, 2003; Komárik, 2003, and others).

Relatively accurate contours of the character of educational research in the first decade of the new democracy and the beginnings of the history of research in the new Millennium can be produced based on a comprehensive study by Gavora (2004). In his study, he analyzed all the research documented in Slovak's most prestigious scientific pedagogical journal *Pedagogická revue* published between 1993 and 2003. According to him, this period was characterized by serious changes in education under the influence of radical political, economic and social transformations after 1989. These changes were taking place also in the area of organization of research in Slovakia. His analysis of 151 studies indicated the existence of a tension between theoretically grounded and explorative research: The research was mostly explorative (various probes) with little theoretical synthesis. It was primarily motivated by practical needs after 1989, not by theoretical issues, as there was not enough time for that. But, in fact, the same emphasis on explorative research was typical also before 1989. It seemed as though Slovak pedagogy, had time to solve only practical questions, and did not have enough time for thorough, theoretically grounded research, nor for creating groups of co-workers, as it was in the institution Ústav experimentální pedagogiky SAV till 1993.

An overview of studies published in the scientific educational journal *Pedagogika* in the period 1990–2000 was elaborated also by a Czech researcher Mareš (2000). He compared this period with research in 1951–1989. He confirmed that the volume of research grew radically after 1989 (p. 388).

Research of the level of professionalization of the teaching profession has produced evidence that instead of academic development of knowledge or practical training of individual teaching skills, the biggest challenge for TE is to develop the key competencies of the teaching profession. Of course, the concept of teacher competencies is likely to resonate differently in different national contexts. In accordance with the Czech approach (Lukášová – Kantorková, 2003; Vašutová, 2004), in 2006 a Slovak group of experts elaborated a transparent interactional framework of teacher's competencies called *Professional development of teachers* (*Profesijný rozvoj učiteľa*, Kasáčová, Kosová et al, 2006, pp. 44–47), defined as complex combinations of knowledge, skills, understanding, values and attitudes, leading toward effective action in a specific situation. A 'truly' professional teacher is a person who is a) an autonomous expert eager to know himself or herself; b) an expert in developing healthy, functional relations supporting all pupils to blossom as individual personalities; c) an expert capable of teaching that facilitates the learning process; and d) an expert in reflection and self-reflection. Teacher's everyday professional activities are thus focused on a) pupils, b) educational process, and on c) his/her own self-development (Babiaková & Tabačáková, 2009, pp. 179–202). The purpose of this Framework was to ensure that all TE programmes in Slovakia would aim to develop a common core of teaching competencies in their graduates (as recommended by the European Commission), and thus to ensure that teachers will be as prepared as responsible, reflective professionals.

3.3 Categorization of pedeutological research

The 1990s, and especially the beginning of the Millennium, have witnessed a massive increase in pedeutological research in Europe, including Central and Eastern states. Though in Western democracies it was associated with the new phase of neo-professionalism of the teaching profession, in post-communist countries researchers have tried to contribute to solving the still persisting crisis of the teaching profession via their work. E.g. research in Nitra and Prešov showed areas of most serious dissatisfaction among graduates of TE in teaching at the secondary school level (Kosová, 2011, p. 54), namely:

- The high proportion of academics, theory in their TE studies, torn from the educational reality;
- Unpreparedness to work with troubled, disabled, disadvantaged pupils;
- Little training and a lack of teaching skills in how to prepare thematic programs, innovative tools, and classroom work;
- Ignorance of cross-curricular themes.

The goal of this section is not and cannot be an exhaustive overview, but only a draft of its contours indicating significance in pedeutological research during this period, the most common research topics and the categories of completed research, as well as research methods, mainly in both Czech and Slovak Republics. To ensure the clarity of the information, the individual research studies are mentioned only very briefly and they are listed in Charts 7–9.

3.3.1 Categories of research according to research themes

The following lists of research studies, mostly from the first decade of the existence of the Slovak and the Czech Republics (1993–2002), were put together based on the various categorization and data, mainly from Slovak and Czech pedeutological experts Mareš (2000), Kasáčová (2002), Průcha (2002), and Kariková (2005 – from predominantly psychological view at teacher's career).

One of the main resources for their data from the transformation period were the information about successfully completed research grant projects. Here are a few examples of them, carried out by researchers from Czech universities and other research institutions on (Průcha, 2002):

- Changes of the Czech education in European perspective (Kotásek et al,1994–1996);
- The eaching profession and the process of its construction (Štech et al, 1994);
- Primary teacher education (Nelešovská et al, 1995, 2010); on teaching profession as seen by the teachers (Spilková, 1994);
- Methodological principles of primary education (Spilková et al., 1996);
- Support of alternative ways of teaching (Václavík, 1995 & 1997);
- Social and cultural characteristics of future teachers (motivation, economic background, educational background, social background) – (Kotásek & Růžička, 1996; Tichá, 1995 & 1999);
- The role of males/females in the teaching profession;
- The professional activities of teachers on specific educational levels, including kindergarten teachers (Burkovičová, 2006).

The main areas of research in the 1990s could be summarized from the research studies that were published in that period. Mareš (2000) in his overview of educational psychological research on teachers during

1990–2000 in the Czech Republic, stated that this is the period when the emphasis of researchers shifts from students to teachers (p. 388). Related to research on teachers, he found four distinguishable trends to:

- Observe the specific actions of teachers (Pstružinová 1992, Hrdina 1992, Gavora 1994).
- Analyze subjective phenomena associated with teachers (Mareš, Skalská & Kantorková 1994, Bendl 1997), burn-out (Zelinová 1998, Edger & Čermák 2000).
- Research personal features of teacher's character (Novotný 1997).
- Look at teachers from the point of view of students (Semerádová 1994, Rendl 1994, Mareš, Man & Stuchlíková 2000).

After the beginning of the Millennium, one of the most significant trends is the research on the level of teachers' professionalization, specifically on professional knowledge and competencies of teachers (V. Švec et al., 2000, 2002 &2005; Walterová 2001; Spilková - Vašutová 2008 etc.). The results of research so far indicates a growing tendency to retreat from academic teacher preparation and also from mainly practical training of teaching skills. More and more a dominant role of expert knowledge and professional competencies of teachers has been emphasized. What has become vitally important is the investigation of teachers' idea of teaching, their self-efficacy, and their implicit and intuitive ideas of the teaching process, hand in hand with the explicit and well-internalized knowledge of teaching theories. The decisive role of systematic theoretical reflection on practice in designing teacher's personal as well as professional concepts of self-teaching has been proved. A simultaneous, interconnected academic and professional, as well as theoretical and practical preparation of future teachers has been confirmed. The teaching profession can be researched from various angles. One of them is the biodromal development of the professional teacher, of his/her professional career.

Among all the available research directions, special emphasis will be put on raising the professionalism and social status of teachers by researching professional activities of teachers and creating their professiograms.

It would be possible to show that pedeutological research in the last decade proved to be an encouragement and a potentially effective means to disclose some causes of the continuing crisis of teaching profession and finding of the first steps toward the overall awareness of it by more and more teachers in post-communist countries. Kasáčová (2005), in her research of TE students, confirmed evident positive impact of well-organized courses and the increase of capability of self-analysis, ability to apply theory to practice and create own educational methods of future teachers.

The next Charts 7 & 8 represent data on pedeutological research from the biodromal perspective both in Slovakia and in the Czech Republic (categories according to Kariková, 2005).

Chart 7: Pedeutological research on teachers from the biodromal perspective (Slovakia)

The phase of development of teaching professional career		
Researcher Author	**Year of publishing**	**Focus of research**
Motivation and decision for teaching profession		
Krystoň	1994	Pre-preparation for the teaching profession (secondary school students)
Kasáčová	1996,1998	Motivation of future teachers
Kariková	1999,2002	Personality of a future teacher: personal maturity and mental health, cognitive presuppositions, personal aptitude to become a teacher
Valihorová	1995	Psychological aspects of chosing new primary TE students
Gavora	2002	Decision to become a teacher

Preparation for teaching profession		
Kolláriková	1993	Phases of development of teaching profession
Hargašová	1993	Dispensing with illusions
Porubská	1994	Professional orientation and selection of TE students
Schnitzerová	1994,1995	Change of attitudes of TE students
Kasáčová	1996	Expectations of respondents to the study
Žiaková	1996	Adaptation problems of TE students starting their TE study
Kariková	1995, 1999, 2000	Personal characteristics of future teachers
Pašková Valihorová	2008	Performance satisfaction of TE students
Novice adaptation to teaching profession and acceptance of teacher role (usually up to the age of 30)		
Lašek	1995	Novice teachers
Kariková	1996	Psychological personality features
Kasáčová	1998	Novice teachers
Portík	2002	Becoming a novice teacher
Stabilization and identification with teaching profession (usually up to the age 31 – 45)		
Kariková	1998	Evaluation of teachers by teachers/ headmasters
Zelinová	1998	Burnout
Kariková	2005	Research of female teachers of primary schools – their motivation, adaptation, performance, comparison between groups of female teachers – declining interest in teacher education
Stability and ending teaching profession (usually after the age of 46)		
Zelina	1990, 1994	Burnout, pressure
Flešková	1997	Burnout, pressure
Kasáčová	1998	Teachers as experts in their profession
Poliach	1999	Solving problems

Turek, Zeman, Jakubcová	1999	Lifelong teacher education
Doušková, Kasáčová	2002	Experienced teachers
Darák, Ferencová & Šuťáková	2006	Interventions by teachers in the development of pupils' competencies, focused on experiment and explorative research of learning competencies 2005 – 2007 – of pupils, teachers, students of teacher education

Chart 8: Examples of research on teachers from the biodromal perspective (Czech Republic)

The phase of development of teaching professional career		
Researcher author	Year of publishing	Focus of research
Motivation and decision for teaching profession		
Havlík	1995	Motivation of future teachers
Hřebíček	1995	Motivation of future teachers
Musil	1999	Motivation to become a student of teacher education
Preparation for teaching profession		
Mareš	1991	TE student's evaluation of TE studies
Havlík	1998	Ideas of future self-realization
Nezvalová	1994, 2002	Teacher preparation, reflection
Žiaková	1996	Students' adaptation to TE studies
Svatoš	1999, 2002	Reflection in teacher preparation, portfolio
Šimíčková-Čížková	1998	Neurotic manifestations among future teachers
Švec V.	2002	Teacher education
Kantorková Lukášová	1994, 1998 2000, 2006	Teacher preparation (professional precondition, evaluation by students, reflection)

Novice adaptation to teaching profession and acceptance of teacher role (usually up to the age of 30)		
Šimoník	1994	Novice teachers
Kalhous, Horák	1996	Problems of novice teachers
Průcha	1997	Teachers' development
Spilková	1998	Teacher' preparation and development
Štech	1998	Teaching profession
Prokešová	1998,2000	Problems of novice teachers, concerns about future contacts with parents
Stabilization and identification with teaching profession (usually up to the age 31 – 45)		
Langová	1992	Images of pupils about ideal teacher
Kraus	1991	Evaluation of teachers by parents
Chráska	1993	
Rabušincová, Pol	1996	
Střelec	1996	
Průcha	1997	More experienced and responsible teachers, success of teachers
Šimičková	2001	Evaluation of the school environment in connection with the length of teacher practice, satisfaction with teaching profession
Javorská	2002	Personality characteristics of teachers
Stability and ending teaching profession (usually after the age of 46)		
Obdržálek	1991	Time pressure
Slavík, Čapková	1994	Reflection on teaching profession
Kurelová	1998	Burn-out syndrome, stress
Fialová Schneiderová	1998, 2001	Burnout, pressure
Urbánek	1999	Time pressure – beginning and experienced teachers
Havlík	1999	Willingness to stay in a profession
Vašutová, Švecová	1999	The social status of teachers

| Eger, Čermák | 2000 | Burnout |
| Walterová | 2001, 2002 | Specific phenomena of teaching profession |

Chart 9: Research of other specific pedeutological themes suggested by Kasáčová (1998)

Research theme	Slovakia	Czech Republic
Pedagogical thinking of teachers	Gavora 1988	Mareš 1996
Teacher's capabilities and competencies	Kasáčová 1999 Dargová 2001	Spilková 1999 Horká 1999
Social and economic status of teachers Professional satisfaction Life satisfaction of teachers	Valica 2002 Poliaková 2014 Pašková, Valihorová 2009,2010	Paulík 1999 Seberová 2009
Ethics of teaching profession	Žilínek 1997 Samuhelová 1996	
Teacher's personality	Kariková 2005: recently especially feminization in schools, research of female teachers of primary schools – their motivation, adaptation, performance, comparison between groups of female teachers – declining interest in teacher education	
Threatening factors of teacher education –burn out	Zelina 1997, 1998, Hroncová 2001, Valica 2002, Daniel 2002	

Pedagogical communication and its aspects, interaction analysis		Průcha 1995, Mareš 1995 Pstružinová 1992, Svatoš 1995
International comparative research length of preparation, type of institution, age structure, gender structure, activities of teachers (forms, methods, theme preferences), salaries	Kosová 2003	Průcha 1997 Blížkovský et al. 2000
Summary of research studies on teachers' profession 1991 – 1997 by the Institute of information and prognosis in education (Ústav informácií a prognóz školstva);	Beňo et al. 2001	
Professional self-reflection of teachers	Hupková 2006	

A similar approach to the classification of pedeutological research was elaborated by Průcha (2002a) who gave an overview of pedeutological research in the 1990s in the Czech Republic (based on categories reflecting the main topics of ECER – European Conference on Educational Research conferences in 1995–2000):

- Social profiles of students at pedagogical faculties: Kotásek & Růžička 1996;
  - Orientation to the profession of teachers: Havlík 1997;
  - Attitudes of future teachers to their own profession: Urbánek 2000;
  - Analysis of the applicants of the study at the TE tertiary institution: Křesáková 2001;
- Research on teachers education:
  - Analysis of teacher education – identification of basic problems: Spilková (& Uhlířová) 1991, 1992, 1994, 1997;

- Lack of research as the starting point for the transformation in teaching education: Kantorková 1994; Machalová 1994; Nelešovská 1995; Kalous 1994;
- Teacher's skills and competencies: V. Švec et al. 2000, 2002;
- Action research of TE students: disruption of the normative model of study (movement HNUtíSobě, Kaslová, 1994; Spilková 1994 – students want to try their own individual ways in the context of official study; Štech 1994; Lukášová 2004; Janík 2005; V. Švec 2005; Stuchlíková 2006; Nelešovská 2008; Lazarová 2006; Bartošová, Fáberová 2007; Horká 2008;
- Graduates of teacher education – interest in starting their teaching careers: Havlík 1997; Zimová 1997; Hřebíček 1995; Havlík 1998; Spilková 1996: 31% of graduates of primary teacher training and 50% of graduates of secondary teacher education rejected to start to teach (in comparison with just 2,5% of them in the beginning of the 70-ties);
- Novice teachers – disappointments: Šimoník 1994; Píšová 1999; Bendl 2001; their problems – comparison with teachers abroad: Průcha 1997, 2002; Černotová 2000;
- Predominantly psychological issues in teacher research: Teachers burnout Kebza, Šolcová 1998; Průcha 1997, 2002; Fialová & Schneiderová 1998; Stránská & Poledňová 2005; Zelinová 2008 – comparison between Czech and Slovak teachers (lower burnout rates among teachers in the Czech Republic than in Slovakia); Eger & Čermák 2000 – research on teachers' self-evaluation connected with burnout); workload of the teacher: Vašina & Vološková 1998; Řehulka & Řehulková 1998 – professional deformation of teachers; level of neurological pressure on teachers – Čižková et al. 1998; occupational satisfaction of teachers – Paulík 1999 (dissatisfaction of teachers is caused by the inappropriately high demands on teaching profession (that the teacher is not able to fulfill); Solfronk & Urbánek 2000 – more positive level of satisfaction than was predicted; Vašina & Vološková 1998; Mlčák 1998. Several researchers in

the 1990 found out that the level of self-esteem of the then TE students was lower than that of other students (Šimoník 1994; Schnitzerová 1995; also Kariková 1995 & 1998);

- Research on relations between teachers and parents: Rabušincová & Pol 1996;
- Teachers as experts: teaching methods, feminization, teachers' workload and their everyday activities (professiograms) – see below.

Comparison with other countries

More than a quarter of a century after the societal changes in 1989, all post-communist countries have witnessed a massive increase of researched areas associated with the teaching profession, and these have been investigated from multiple angles. To give evidence of this, Appendix No. 4 has been added to this publication. It consists of an overview of examples of pedeutological research completed in several European post-communist countries, published since 2003 in the international scientific journal, *The New Educational Review*.

Thanks to several international projects, supported, for instance by EU funds, the way toward availability of data on pedeutological research has been opened wide. Particularly important are the opportunities to find out more comparable data about other post-communist countries. "For researchers investigating deeper meanings of social changes in Central-Eastern European countries, it is essential to study jointly the history of nations living together in this area and most importantly, the educational dilemmas of the present." (Puzstai & Engler, 2014, Preface). There would be quite a few opportunities to build a study like this just based on the analysis of these available data, but that is not the main purpose of this publication.

To give an example of a joint project of research on teachers, let us mention one successful international research project, carried out by a group of researchers from all four Visegrad countries (Poland, Slovakia,

Hungary and the Czech Republic), supported by the European Visegrad Fund in 2013–2014 (Pusztai & Engler 2014b). The researching team believed that their comparative research activities would lead to the importance of self-reflection in the mirror of all national research initiatives: "We should think together with people living in similar social and economic circumstances instead of looking at our reflection in the mirror of the West, which has a highly simplified idolized image in our minds and a thought system different from our own" (*Preface to the Project*).

Results of this comparative project were published in two collections of research studies involving data about teachers not just from Visegrad, but also from other countries, predominantly previous communist countries. One of them (Pusztai & Engler eds., 2014a) deals with recent information on the research of teachers in the stage of their preparation at TE institutions. It includes a study on motivation of HE students – future teachers in Poland, the process of choosing the teaching profession and the commitment to teaching of TE students in Hungary, research on teacher education in Romania and Hungary, etc. Though the focus of all the studies is the same – research on various phases of teacher's career, this collection of papers is a very good means to compare different research procedures or methods. Their results might be of particular interest to those wanting to know what has been researched already. For instance, research on most post-communist countries confirms evidence of the low social status of teachers, especially in comparison to the professional character of the activities they carry out during the performance of their job. On the other hand, a study from Spain shows that Spanish society considers primary education teachers as having the second highest social status right after medical doctors (Aparicio & Arévalo 2014, p. 41).

In the second mentioned volume (Pusztai & Engler eds., 2014b), comparative research on further issues of teachers' development are presented – on the past and current prestige and social construction of the teaching profession (Hungary, Poland, Slovakia), on recruitment of students (Hungary and Poland), on the knowledge of future teachers (USA, Taiwan, Germany), on the role of social networks in the well-being of TE students (Hungary and Romania), on TE students' goals, values and future plans (Hungary, Poland, Slovakia), on multiculturalism of TE students, teacher burn-out, etc. The researchers (Fónai, Dusa & Moldová Chovancová 2014, pp. 88–89) confirmed that the "social status of teachers is deteriorating on the basis of income, and social prestige". Low financial appreciation of teachers' work was confirmed in Poland, Hungary and Slovakia.

Thanks to the initiative of researchers from Debrecen University in Hungary, in 2012 a new network called TECERN (Teacher Education Central Europe Research Network) was created for the purpose of mutual cooperation and joint investigations on issues connected with the teaching profession, their TE preparation or their social status. In their recent publication (Pusztai, Engler & Markóczi, 2015), researchers from this region admitted that though they have realized that there have been some common characteristics in the cultural and societal context of TE preparation of their teachers, they are also aware of the lack of knowledge about each other's research results (p. 7). This publication consists of three key sets of data on pedeutological research – studies on wider cultural and societal context of TE, on specifics of TE adequate to specific needs of present students and schools, and finally on the new trends and challenges of teaching profession.

Recently another publication (Pusztai, Meglédi et al, 2015) by researchers coming from the post-communist countries located in the Carpathian Basin was produced to allow comparison of research on teachers among even wider group of post-communist countries (Hungary, Romania, Serbia, Ukraine, Slovakia, and Poland). In their collection of studies focused primarily on students' decisions for the teaching profession and on teacher education (Pusztai & Meglédi, 2015), researchers in the last decade have been focusing on investigating the characteristics of TE students, their commitment on career and issues connected with their university preparation, on the effects of educational reforms upon teachers and their education, on learning conditions of TE for students from minor communities, TE students' leisure activities and state of health.

In order to compare the research themes in the post-communist European region with other democratic countries in the 1990s, it might be useful to compare them with the research themes in the 1990's worldwide as summarized in the fourth edition of the *AERA Handbook* (Richardson, 2001). In their research overviews, the authors pointed to the emphasis in research on education as a process and the new phenomena that penetrated into education. They represented a variety of legitimized educational perspectives, predominantly constructivist, socio-cultural and critical perspectives. The *Handbook* gives a picture of the new trends and emphases on new research themes, such as dialogue, human rights and social justice, diversity, holistic approaches, culture, dialogue, social justice, etc. A typical example would be a research on the impact of multiplicity and ethnic diversity on the educational process. The second topic that appears most repeatedly in research was the teaching content of school subjects.

The scope of topics in the fourth edition of the *AERA Handbook* is very wide, including analysis of theoretical grounds of high quality scientific research (traditional approaches to research on teaching). But it also includes themes associated with the appropriate use of various research methods, especially of qualitative methods such as ethnography, validity, narratives, or a combination of social inquiry research methods.

As for specifics of research on teachers and their profession, besides the above-mentioned topics, the researchers were focusing on teachers' role as agents of change in culturally changing classrooms. Of course, the perpetually significant question of the multidimensional relationships of teachers was also widely presented in the research studies. According to its editor, Richardson, the *2001 AERA Handbook* represented a far broader perspective on teachers, learners, community and culture than had previous editions of the *Handbook*.

For a more complete picture of the years around and after the beginning of the Millennium, let us briefly remind another reference publication – the *International Handbook of Research on Teachers and Teaching* written by British, Australian and American educational experts (eds. L. J. Saha, A. G. Dworkin, 2009). The authors present research on teachers which was carried out during the end of the 20th century and in the first decade of the 21st century. This collection of research studies brings evidence of overlaps between the themes of current research in post-communist countries and research in other developed countries. What is evident from this list is the common emphasis on the phases of teacher's professional career and its stages, as was mentioned in the Charts 7 & 8 viewing research on teachers from the biodromal perspective. What follows is an overview of all areas of research according to this *Handbook* (eds. Saha & Dworking, 2009), as used by the editors and authors. The purpose for including this is to show a wider whole-world framework that could be viewed as a reference framework for evaluation the regional research:

- Introduction to pedeutological research: teachers as researchers, the character of research on teachers, trends in pedeutology as a science and also in educational systems, new trends in research methodology;

- The process of teacher preparation: research of TE preparation of students in TE programmes including the role of mentors, levels of study and credentials; recruitment and stamina in the teaching performance, the life-long continuing education of teachers;

- Various characteristics of teachers: their social status, political orientations, their knowledge and skills, their values, teaching and management styles, the influence of diversity upon their performance;

- Teacher behavior: in the classroom, their relationships in the teaching team, toward school management, students and parents; their commitment, their beliefs regarding learning, their work with textbooks, their emotional world, features and reasons of teacher's misbehavior and of mistreatment of teachers;

- Teachers' life-long career in a biodromal perspective: tracking teachers, balance between work, power and authority; teachers' salaries and benefits, burnout and teacher's resilience, the teacher and promotion;
- Comparative perspective on teachers: teachers in diverse classrooms and cultures;
- Dimensions of teaching: teachers' styles, models, diversity, creativity, ethics and teaching, teachers' expectations and labeling,
- The process of teaching in the classroom: teacher-student interaction, assessment and examinations, classroom management, teachers as role models, teaching in a multicultural classroom, teaching in different-size classes, the use of ICT, effective teaching, teaching and nonverbal behavior in the classroom;
- Teaching specific groups of students: secondary (vocational) and tertiary level, students with special needs, teaching gifted and talented children, teaching mixed-gender classes, the problem of boy's achievements in schools;
- The ways of teaching of individual subjects;
- The challenges in the teaching profession: issues of tracking pupils, testing and teaching to tests, value-added models of teachers' effects, teaching during educational reforms, grade retention redux, teaching in an era of heightened school accountability.

Comparing the list of researched areas in the *International Handbook* with Slovak and Czech as well as with the Appendix No. 5, it is evident that:

- As for the research problems and research areas completed by Slovak and Czech researchers, all research areas would fit into the framework of international research perspective. Though the authors of this *Handbook* obviously did not work with data on the Czech Republic or Slovakia – as there is only one mention of Czech teachers' salaries and no comment on Slovakia – they could be incorporated into this published overview of research topics characterizing research during the period around the turn of the 3rd millennium

- Of course, not all topics mentioned in this *Handbook* are covered in the Slovak and Czech research. Each country and region has its own specific topics due to the specifics of its culture, history etc. E.g. when speaking about researching diversity in the classroom, in the Slovak research there has been more effort invested in researching the education of ethnic minorities (namely Roma minority) than religious plurality, as Slovakia has had the history of mono-religious Christian country (80% Christians in 2011, then only about 1000 members of Bahai's faith and no other registered religious group). Several high-interest research topics mentioned in the *Handbook* are also the biggest challenges for the current pedeutological research in Slovakia, e.g. the effect of educational transformation on teachers and students.

Individual research studies focused on teachers in various countries reflect miscellaneous educational, but also wider social issues, problems, or challenges. Investigations into the teaching profession which were implemented into the national curricula or standards of the teaching profession or even into the international educational policy documents are of exceptionally significant value for the international community of teachers. In the Appendix No. 5 Hanesová collected some examples of individual and institutional research projects that have been connected to at least to some extent –with research on the teaching profession, teachers' activities or the status of teachers (2009).

Professiography of teachers

Though, generally, research on teachers is a very fertile area of scientific work and there has been a lot of research carried out both in Slovakia and the Czech Republic, the area of systematic **professiography of teaching profession**, i.e. **of professional activities of teachers,** was an abiding interest of pedeutological researchers. It has been more intensively studied only in the very recent years.

Let us start the overview with *three comparative professiography research studies using comparison* of data among several countries. One of the first serious comparative professiography studies, was a study by Blížkovský, Kučerová, and Kurelová (2000), who focused on professional activities and working conditions of teachers in the Czech Republic, Slovak Republic and Poland. In its substance, it was independent research, including research on teacher's working time. Professiograms of Czech primary teachers showed that they work about 45–46 hours a week (similar to 2400 Swiss teachers – Landert's results in 1999: 42–45 hours a week): 1/3 of this is teaching, 1/3 activities connected with teaching (preparation for teaching, correcting assignments) and other activities.

Later in (2005), in his study, Janik described some aspects of the reality of professional activities of teachers in primary school in Austria, the Czech Republic, Slovakia, Hungary, and Slovenia).

One of the most recent comparative professiographic studies, called *The Profession of Pre-primary teacher and Primary Teacher within a Dynamic Concept*, was carried out by an international team of researchers from three faculties (the Faculty of Education at Matej Bel University in Banská Bystrica, Slovakia, the Faculty of Pedagogy and Psychology at the University Kazimierza Wielkiego in Bydgoszcz, Poland and the Faculty of Pedagogy at the University of Ostrava in Ostrava, the Czech Republic) under the Slovak leadership of Kasáčová in 2008–2010. According to her analysis (2009, pp. 20–38), the image of the teaching profession had been for a long time based mainly on 'intuition', and not on scientific research. This was especially true in the case of pre-primary and primary teaching profession. The team completed thorough research on pre-primary and primary teachers' activities, and thus succeeded in creating their professiograms. The plan was to uncover the discrepancies between pedeutological theory and the required competencies of teachers. These were defined in the document *Competence Profile of the Pedagogical Employee with their everyday practice*. It involved also teachers' competence to organize daily activities (Kasáčová et al, 2006). The activities that were being investigated could have been both directly and indirectly connected to the process of education, especially the pedagogical thinking of teachers, pedagogical communication, pedagogical capabilities and competencies of teachers and specific real professional activities. Besides their own research, the members of this research team prepared bibliographies of publications on pedeutological research in their countries (2009):

- Kasáčová, Cabanová, & Babiaková – research on primary teachers (Slovakia);
- Jarešová – research on pre-primary teachers (Slovakia);
- Seberová – research on primary teacher (Czech Republic) ;
- Burkovičová – research on pre-primary teacher (Czech Republic) ;
- Nowak – research on pre-primary and primary Polish teacher 1980–2009.

More details on the results of the above-mentioned comparative professiographic research in 2008–2010 appear in chapter 4.3.

Chart 10: Other research studies focused on professiography themes in the Slovak Republic

Examples of professiography in the Slovak Republic after 1989	Researcher	Year
Research on teachers' profession (analysis of opinion, feelings, attitudes, problems	M. Beňo et al.	1991–1997
Microanalysis of lessons focused on teachers' strategies, teaching styles	Zelina	1994
Effort to create professiography: opinions of teachers on teaching profession in Slovakia – stress, salaries, social status	Fülöpová	1998
Multiple researched issues	Kasáčová et al.	since 1999
Life stories of teachers (motivation, teacher's career, factors of influence);	Gavora	2001, 2002
Biodromal development of teachers' career, burnout, psychological view of teacher personality, teachers' attitudes, motivation, satisfaction etc.; psychological aspects of teacher activities (burn-out)	Kariková	2002, 2005
Research on teachers and their competencies	Gavora	2007
Teachers' opinions and expectations from their own professional education.	Babiaková	2008
Further education of teacher in order to develop competencies of a supervising teacher	Černotová	2006
Experimental verification of the quality of professional training of students during their internship in order to raise its quality	Doušková	2004, 2007

Other research studies focused on professiography themes in the Czech Republic

To list Czech authors presenting professiography and specific examples of multiple research in the Czech Republic, first, let us mention Průcha (e.g. 2002) with his repertories of 'actual' activities of teachers, Vašutová (2001) with her bibliography of studies on the teaching profession, and Havlík (2000) who carried out research of teachers' education. Also the following researchers focused on various professiographic topics.

Chart 11: Examples of professiography in the Czech Republic after 1989

Studies	Researcher	Year
The problems of novice teachers with selected professional activities	Šimoník	1994, 1995
Multiple researched issues	Průcha	since 1980s
Multiple researched issues: (1991–1994, 1995–1998) – workload of teachers, weaknesses and strong sides of teaching profession, analysis of lessons, comparative professiogram. The aim: to study teachers' competence, to define the standards, optimization of pre-graduate education of teachers	Blížkovský	since 1980s–
Level of difficulty of professional activities	Bendl	1997
Burn-out of teachers	Kebza, Šolcová	1998
Professiogram	Kurelová	1997 2004
Professional work load of primary teachers – professional work load of primary teachers (a weekly observation recording sheet)	Urbánek	1999 2001 2005
Teachers' activities, action research – implementation of innovative strategies (participated observation, thorough interview of teachers and their implementation of innovative educational strategies	Kasíková	1995 2002
Factors and context of development of teachers professional competences	Havel, Vlčková	2004

Reflection of problems with professional activities, problems with professional activities	Chráska, Klapal	2004
Comparative professiography at primary schools – video studies and analysis of teachers' activities while implementing the curriculum in schools	Janik	2005 2009
Research on teachers' profession 1999 – 2007: reflection of demanding professional situation, evaluation of profession, analysis of professional activities, model of professional standard for teachers	Vašutová	1999 – 2007
Teachers of preparatory classes – life stories of teachers of preparatory classes in *focus groups*	Nemec	2005
Inventory for teachers' professional assessment, teachers' activities for professional evaluation and self-reflection Competence of reflection of the teaching process	Heřmanová, Langová Slavík, Siňor	2005 1993
Mental pressure of teaching profession	Rehulka	2005
Teaching profession and changing educational demands	Spilková	1997 2007
Standardization of teachers' professional activities	Rýdl	2008
Teachers build their teacher's identity – life stories	Svariček	2007
Phenomenological approach to professiography	Stuchlíková	2006
Phenomenological approach to professiography	Gőbelová	2006
Video-studies and analysis of teachers' activities	Janik	2005, 2009

Ways of building teacher's identity – teacher's life history of construction of teaching profession identity from novices to experts	Švaříček	2007
Teachers self-reflection „Me and my profession"(motivation, cognition, emotions)	Juklová	2008

Comparison with other countries

Professiographic research has been recognized as more and more significant for the development of the theory and practice of pedeutology and not only in post-communist countries, but in the wider European and global contexts as well. It is evident for example, from the fourth edition of the *AERA Handbook* (Richardson, 2001), which confirmed the shift of research from investigating changes influencing schools to the researching educational process in schools, real life in the classrooms, and the activities of teachers and their correlations. The authors verbalized their effort to search out the best solutions in order to secure academic success for all children. On the other hand, a substantial number of studies confirms that many educational problems derive from deficient conditions outside the school. Other pieces of evidence and examples of overlap of the emphasis on professiographic research in various and educational systems regions were collected by Hanesová in 2009 (see Appendix No. 5).

3.3.2 Methods used in pedeutological research after 1989

The increase in the number of educational research topics and researching teams was accompanied by an enlarged inventory of pedeutological research methods, creating the continuum of quantitative-qualitative research methodology. The expansion of the number and diversity of pedeutological research after 1993, especially after the beginning of the third Millennium, has been particularly evident in the countries with previously limited research maneuvering area. The period after 1989 has been characterized by an unprecedented tendency to adopt in research practice research methods from Western countries.

Mareš in his overview of 50 years of research published in the journal *Pedagogika* (2000), underlined a new trend in educational research methodology after 1989. He describes a tendency to accomplish research with much smaller research samples, using qualitative methods more often (especially thorough interviews, not forgetting particular phenomenological interview – Osuská & Pupala, 1996) though often in coexistence with classical empirical research on wide samples. Among the newest research methods there is a projective method, used predominantly in qualitative research (Mareš, 2000, p. 390). As for the statistical methods, both procedures typical for qualitative research and quantitative statistical methods, especially descriptive statistics have been used.

Gavora, in his study (1994) based on an analysis of 10 volumes (1993–2003) of a scientific journal *Pedagogická revue* published in Slovakia, compared the ratio of the amount of various types of educational research methods. The results of this comparison showed that 60% of researchers used quantitative research methods, 37% historic research method, and only 3% qualitative research out of which 62% studies were describing situation, 20% were experimental, 16% evaluative studies and 2% correlative studies. The most often used research methods were questionnaires, then interviews, counting of semantic differential, quantitative contest analysis, analysis of products other than texts, and observations. The weakest point of the research completed was little attention paid to issues of validity or reliability.

To summarize his investigation, Gavora (2004) commented that educational research in Slovakia in the period 1993–2003 was characteristic by a prevalence of explorative research, a considerable amount of quantitative research, good presentation of historic research, but a deficit of qualitative research. The following list presents examples of research methods used in the first years after 1989 in Slovakia and the Czech Republic:

- Observations of pedagogical communication and interaction, observation systems, observation scales, etc. (1993, 1996);
- Interview (1993, 1996);
- Questionnaires (1990, 1995, 1996);
- Projective method (1992, 1997);
- Experiments (1991, 1993, 1994);
- Casuistry (1991, 1992);
- Action research (1996, 1997);
- Method of verbal statements – discourse analysis (2002);
- New tendencies of research methodology: historical ethnography of education – study of oral history/life stories (life history, oral history, informal narratives, personal narration) of teachers (1992, 1996, 1999, 2002), school ethnography (1992, 1993, 1994).

The following Chart 12 shows which prevailing methods in pedeutology were used by Czech and Slovak researchers before 1989 and after 1989 (emphasis expressed by bold font).

Chart 12: Main research methods before 1989 and after 1989

Main research methods before 1989	**Main research methods after 1989**
Observations of lessons	*Observations of lessons*
Interviews (mainly in the 1950s and 1960s)	*Interviews*
Questionnaires – starting in the 1970s	***Questionnaires***
EXPERIMENTS	***Experiments*** *(1990s) – fewer than before*
Prognostic methods	*Prognostic methods*
Casuistry	*Casuistry*

Historical ethnography of education – study of oral history	**Historical ethnography of education – study of oral history**
Action research	Action research
Didactic tests (dominant in 1950s & 1960s)	Method of verbal statements (utterances)
Interactional analysis (1970s), audio recording	Projective method
Psycho-diagnostic tests on teachers	School ethnography

Comparison with other countries

Thanks to all these changes in the post-communist world, but also due to globalization, international exchanges, unprecedented technological and internet support, the awareness of different research methods has spread across European states, regardless of their history (e.g. via accessible reference books, such as six editions of *Research Methods in Education* by Cohen, Manion & Morrison (6th edition in 2007). As shown in the immediately preceding paragraphs and examples of research themes and methods, it is no longer as simple to navigate among them. Thorough studies have been published on quantitative or qualitative research paradigms and on specific methods, often in multiple versions in one region. In the book market, there are many publications on research methodology in national languages.

So at first glance, it seems that there is no sense anymore in comparing the differences between the research methodologies used by various groups of countries. But we believe that an important question remains related to research methods – the level of quality of their applications. This level, depends, for example, on external factors such as the availability of sufficient financial and institutional support. For these and other reasons relating, for instance, to human resources, we can talk about various qualities of research outputs. This applies to all countries without difference.

The risk of the low level of some research studies is mentioned by the fourth edition of the *AERA Handbook* (Richardson, 2001), describing research methodology used in pedeutology, mainly by Western researchers in the 1990s. At first, they confirm the fact that qualitative research methods in educational sciences ceased to be 'new' to the researchers. On the other hand, the wide range of various research studies, including ethnographic studies, case studies, descriptive narratives, clinical studies, biographies and autobiographies presented in this edition of *AERA Handbook* also points to potential dangers connected with qualitative research. It brings evidence of the low scientific quality of a large amount of qualitative research studies which began "to give some forms of qualitative research a bad name" (LeCompte, p. 43). So this *Handbook* also proposes a way out of this negative state, and that is a wider use of a combination of qualitative and quantitative research methods, as well as repeated emphasis on quantitative methodology. This warning can be very well applied to the research activities in the previously Soviet bloc countries.

Another emphasis of modern pedeutological research that came to the fore in this *AERA Handbook* and which can be applied in all countries, is the need to put more emphasis on the evaluation of the epistemological paradigms, the issues of purpose, including the, "validity of research, changes in ethnographic research due to diverse approaches to the concept of culture", etc. (LeCompte, 2009).

As analyses of resent research reports, scientific journals, conference proceedings shows, researchers in transition countries deal with similar methodological issues, as were described in the fourth edition of the *AERA Handbook* (Richardson, 2001):

- Philosophical approaches, critical issues and current trends and the possible future of quantitative research;
- Reconsideration of research paradigms in education;
- Changing the conceptions of culture and ethnographic methodology;

- Uses of narrative research on school practice;
- Importance of validity of qualitative research;
- The trend of mixing research methodologies;
- Realizing advances in assessment;
- Significant role of action research.

Traces of these methodological trends can be found in several national and international educational journals, published in the Eastern and Central European countries (e.g. in Czech-Polish-Slovak international journal, the *New Educational Review*, published in the English language).

4

Examples of pedeutological research

In this last chapter, we present more comprehensive studies of selected research areas, such as the recruitment and retention of TE students and teachers, feminization in education, and the professional activities of teachers. These findings were presented and published by the author of this book in three conference papers collections. The reason for doing so again – with the permission of their editors – in this publication is to document not only the current trends in researching methodology in these three areas but also their results. For more details on these research topics see the mentioned studies (Hanesová 2014, 2015a, & 2015b).

4.1 Research on the recruitment of future teachers and their stamina

Recruitment of teachers can be viewed from wider or narrower angle. In its wider sense, recruitment is a process consisting of several steps, from the information campaign, through the entrance exams and intake policies and the open day presentations of the TE faculties to the applicants, to the acceptance of the best prospective students. These activities are carried out by the government and by TE faculties. Slovakia belongs to that group of countries that apply 'open recruitment' of teachers, which means that recruitment management is decentralized. It is the responsibility of individual schools or local authorities (internet source of Eurydice).

Teacher recruitment can be also viewed from a narrower angle as the research area focused on analyzing the profile of the population of young people who want to study or are already studying TE (Průcha,

1997, p. 202). It focuses on discussing one's abilities, motivation, and processes preceding the decision to become a teacher. It is connected with students' extrinsic and intrinsic motivation, their decision to study at a TE faculty, retention to stay focused on teaching profession during actual TE preparation in spite of its frustrations and weaknesses, and the final decision to take a school teaching position.

It seems that the current non-attractiveness of the teaching profession is reflected in the lower numbers of applicants for TE as well as in the rising number of teachers leaving the profession, especially younger teachers (Kosová, 2011, p. 9). Similarly to most of the EU countries, the Slovak education system faces a double challenge of **teachers' recruitment**: how to enlarge the pool of applicants for TE, and how to also tighten the criteria for selecting people for teaching posts.

Research on teacher recruitment during 1990–2004

After the democratic revolutions of 1989, research on teachers stopped playing the role of propaganda and a new concept of free research was born. Several theoretical publications offering advice on how to carry out proper research were published. An important summary of overall pedeutological research in the first era of Slovak democracy was published by Gavora (2004) in the Slovak research journal *Pedagogická Revue*. Our overview of research on teacher education recruitment is presented in Charts 13 a 14.

Chart 13: Research on TE recruitment in Slovakia during 1993–2004

Researcher	Focus/sample	Main purpose/result
Porubská 1990-1993	Decisions to study TE by students (for ISCED1)	51.4% decide for T profession during the age 6–15 38.8% decide during higher secondary school Big influence of family background on choosing teaching position (43% have teachers in family)
Schnitzerová 1994	TE students' attitudes toward teaching	Decline of positive attitude from 1st to 4th grade in TE
Krystoň 1994	Decisions for TE of secondary school students	Teaching profession was considered to be the third most attractive (out of seven suggested): 54% of girls and 39% of boys.
Kasáčová 1995,1996	Motivation for TE, TE students' expectations from the study	Desire to become a teacher since childhood (44.6%) – to take care of children, to teach them; Influence of a parent – teacher – or both parents are teachers (15.4%); Secondary school of education (ISCED 3); influence of a specific teacher 8.5%; First desire to study something else, but then content with the profession/willing to stay at school the whole life 18.5%.
Kasáčová 2002	Motivation to become a primary school teacher	*2nd grade students* attracted by working with children (55%); the advantages of a teaching job (9%); organizing children and grading (5%); "I do not want to teach after my graduation" (1 student). *3rd grade students* attracted by working with children (only 36%); the advantages of teaching job (1.2%); organizing children and grading (5%); "I do not want to teach after my graduation."(24%)

Gavora 2001	Motives of TE students via life stories	The most important factors: family surrounding during the time of childhood; personality features of the student; experiences from school; role models; key people; life crises.
Gavora 2002	Motives of TE students via life stories	Family background, personal characteristics, experiences from school, role models, key persons and critical events of mid- and late career teachers
Kasáčová 2004	Primary and secondary choices of T profession Motives	5–23% came to study knowing they will never teach but that this is a means to other professions. 64% already working in education, need qualifications Main motives: love of children, experiences with educational work Others: desire to be with interesting people, to have more social contacts. 23% the fulfilment of their life desire

Chart 14: Research of psychological perspective of TE recruitment (Slovakia) 1993–2004

Researcher	Focus/sample	Main purpose/result
Kariková 1998	TE students: evaluation of psychological preparation at TE faculty	Absence of activities focused on solving problems and conflict situations in the classroom. Lack of training for social skills as well as activities focused on better self-recognition and the recognition/understanding of others.
Kariková 1998–1999	Opinions of TE students: listing the skills of an ideal teacher, comparison with opinions of in-service teachers.	Personal maturity and mental health of TE students. An ideal teacher should be fair, creative, and full of empathy, be able to help pupils and listen to them, friendly. Real picture of teachers: they consider themselves to be 1) friendly, 2) able to help pupils, 3) able to appreciate pupils, interested in people, 4) fair and accepting, and 5) emphatic.
Kariková 2000	Personal characteristics of TE students	Social skills: 1/2 of TE students – very little confidence in social situations, 1/3 – problems in expressing emotional proximity/relationships with people. Emotions: more than 1/3 of TE students seem to be restless, unstable, ¼ of them – significantly strained, prone to impatience.
Kariková 2000	Choice of the job by TE students and future economists	Identical numbers of students in both groups (77.3% and 78%) considered their choice of future job as primary one. No evidence of 'attractiveness'/ 'prestige' of economic studies.

Kariková 2000/2001	Stamina – willingness to stay in the profession after the studies	Women: 1/3 of TE students want to go to work abroad (to acquire the language competencies), then return to their profession. Some want to continue to study another (related) field of study (e.g. special education). All men want to find a more profitable job, especially those who are married or are going to get married. Most of them would like to find a job with the police department.
Kariková 2004	Factors influencing the relationship toward the T profession. Motives and worries of TE students. Comparison between teachers and TE students.	Research of anamnestic data, motivation, worries before entering the practice, demands/difficulty, content, fluctuating tendencies. Personal aptitude: for 68% being a teacher was a primary choice. Decisive motive: the opportunity to work with children. Falling interest in studying primary TE. The % of teachers who consider leaving educational sphere is highest among the youngest teachers.
Kariková 2010: comparison with Špendla 1974	Spontaneous interest in teaching profession, positive/ negative sides of T profession	Raising level of feminization, lowering status of teaching profession, growing pressure from negative sides of teaching profession (fear of working with problematic children, communication with parents, legislative changes). Falling interest in studying primary TE.

Compared with Slovak results, Czech research showed similar tendencies in all areas of TE recruitment (Průcha, 2002, pp. 167–168). After 1990, the Czech researchers focused also specifically on investigating the level of interest amongst young people in a teaching career and the motivation to study at a TE institution (e.g. Šimoník, 1994; Chráska, 1996; Kalhous & Horák, 1996; Hřebíček, 1995). Research studies were collected in the Proceedings *Teacher-Preparation and Requirements of School Practice* (1994).

Havlík (1995) aimed at discovering the motives of TE applicants. Many of them did not really mean to study TE in the first place and, in the end, only 58% of them started a TE program. Women, primary education applicants, and students from smaller towns and villages showed higher interest in TE studies. Almost 60% of applicants made their decision shortly before filling out the application. Their last minute motivation proved to be the weakest. Only 36% of TE students would prefer to study TE again. Havlík also investigated the professional perspectives of TE students. About 69% respondents wanted to become teachers. Men were less oriented toward the performance of their studied profession. A family teaching tradition seemed to be relatively strong.

Kotásek with Růžička (1996) and Tichá (1995, 1999) studied the social characteristics of primary TE students, focusing on motivation and on economic, educational and social background. A majority of their parents were administrative and manual workers. Their research, similarly to Havlík's, indicated certain generational continuation in the teaching profession. The main attraction of the teaching profession was the opportunity to educate somebody. A strong influence of middle-European school tradition, especially emphasizing the standards of general knowledge or relatively high levels of social pressures at schools was indicated. In 1996, the social profile of TE students in the Czech Republic showed that they came from a lower social class (34 % of fathers and 27% of mothers are workers) more often than students of other faculties. Up to 23% of TE students came from families with teachers.

More data comparing motivation and opinions of Slovak, Czech and Polish teachers from this era were summarized in the research study *Central-European teacher on the threshold of society – learning community in the beginning of 21st century* (1999), which will be referred to later on (Blížkovský et al., 2000).

Research on teacher recruitment during 2004–2013

In Slovakia the research so far has concentrated on TE students' expectations from their teaching studies, on changes in their attitudes influenced by the studies, on personality preconditions for the performance of the profession, on their willingness to work as a teacher after studies, forming one's professional identity, developing one's reflexivity in the course of preparation for the job, and building one's teaching capabilities.

Similarly to the previous period, Chart 15 mentions some research projects that have taken place at Slovak universities recently.

Chart 15: Research on TE recruitment in Slovakia (2005–2013)

Researcher	Focus/sample	Main purpose/result
Valicová 2006	Motives – primary and secondary choice of teaching profession	Primary choice for 81% (I like to work with children, I want to educate somebody.) Secondary choice for 19% of respondents.
Valkovičová 2008	Motivation of primary teachers: Would you choose TE again?	1/3 respondents – positive response, 2/3 – do not know, changed their minds (reason: finances)
Hrubišková, Višváder 2011	Socio-cultural background of science TE students	To be a science teacher is preferred more by students from rural areas; active believers; often being first born children. ¼ of them do not plan to teach after graduation.

As the overview of research in Slovakia shows, the main motivating factors influencing the decision to become a teacher have been: family influence (especially during the time of childhood), personality features of TE students, the influence of previous teachers of TE students, school experience, role models, key people, critical life periods, and the influence of peers and their altruistic motives.

In the Czech Republic, the interest of young people in the teaching profession is relatively high. On the other hand, some teachers leave their profession, mainly because of low salaries. So the question of recruitment has been the interest of several researchers there too. Seberová (2009, p. 204) highlighted the importance of three monographs summarizing research on TE students and teachers written by Průcha's (2002); Vašutová (2001); and Havlík (2000). Similar to Slovak researcher Gavora (2002), a few Czech researchers apply qualitative methods of teachers' life stories out of which the attitudes of future teachers to their own profession are inferred (Urbánek, 2001). Juklová (2008) used another qualitative method which is the analysis of written self-reflections to suggest factors influencing the development of motivation toward a teaching profession.

4.1.1 Advantages/disadvantages of the teaching profession

In the years 1996–1997, an extensive comparative research by the name of *The Central European Teacher on the Threshold of Society – the Learning Community in the Beginning of the 21st Century* was carried out. Its purpose was to compare the working conditions for the teachers from Poland, Czech Republic and Slovakia before entering the 21st century. The comparison of opinions of teachers on advantages and disadvantages of the teaching profession is presented in Chart 16 and 17 (according to Blížkovský & Kučerová & Kurelová, 2000).

Chart 16: Advantages of teaching profession

Advantages:	Slovakia	Czech Republic (ratio)	Poland (ratio)
Inspiration to work with children and young people	62.7%	26%	25.4%
Longer holidays	39.5%	20.05%	23.9%
Creative work	32.2%	15.85%	
Chance to educate somebody	24.3%	3.46%	
Self-realization	19.2%	12.38%	
Shorter time spent at the work place	19.2%	15.36%	9.4%
Self-education	15.3%	3.46%	
Stable working place	4%	2.97%	
Other reasons	10.7%		19.7%
No advantages			19.7%

Chart 17: Disadvantages of teaching profession

Disadvantages:	Slovakia	Czech Republic (ratio)	Poland (ratio)
Low salary	79.1%	36%	27.4%
Low social status	49.7%	26,89%	12.4%
Psychologically demanding, stress	41.8%	19,33%	15.4%
Poor material equipment	17.5%	4,23%	
Timing, discrepancy holidays	15.3%	3,02%	
Take home work	6.2%	3,93%	
Difficult cooperation with parents	5.1%		
Health problems	5.6%		
Meaningless work/activities	4.5%		
Low competencies of teachers	3.9 %		
Little support for continuous education	2.8 %		
Bad concept of schooling		6.34%	
No problems			12.9%

In the Slovak research group, the negative sides prevailed over positive ones. A strong frustration was caused by low public opinions on teachers, and the financial and moral underestimation of their work. Up to 21.9% would not have chosen the teaching profession again. In the Czech and Polish samples, teachers saw their profession as having balanced advantages and disadvantages. Most Polish teachers would choose their profession again.

From the long-term point of view, an important comparison of teachers' motivation of was carried out by Kariková (2010, pp. 64–66) who used the same questionnaire used in Czechoslovakia by Špendla in 1974. The comparison of statements of teachers in 1974 and in 2009 depicted pros and cons of the teaching profession and why the TE students planned/did not want to start teaching. Almost half of the respondents in 2009 were most concerned about their ability to deal with the behavior of current students, in 1974 their number was very small (4%). The second strongest concern (29%) of 2009 group was the fear of communication with parents which was indicated only by 3% in 1974. The frustration from frequent changes of legislation was pointed at by 19% of respondents in 2009 whereas only 1.5% of them in 1974.

Both researchers found out three categories of positive sides of the teaching profession. The first category consisted of ***psychological*** responses; for instance, respondents liked to work with children and young people. The second category was formed by ***utilitarian*** answers (long holidays, and suitable working hours). Only the group in 1974 was content with the good salary. The third category of positives of teaching profession showed their connection with the ***personal*** character of respondents: ability to see an opportunity to expand their knowledge and to work intellectually. The difference here was the biggest. Current TE students are less interested in the personal benefit of the teaching profession/self-development/continuous education; they do not emphasize the utilitarian sides of the teaching profession.

4.1.2 Factors influencing the decision for the teaching profession

As Kariková (2010) detected in her comparison of the research in 1974 and in 2009, the spontaneous interest in 'becoming a teacher' has had a decreasing tendency. Though the primary choice of the teaching profession seemed similar to the sample in 1974, almost 30% of current teachers would choose another profession if given a second chance. So what factors influence this decision?

According to the above-described previous research, a person's decision for TE studies and teaching profession seems to be influenced by gender, family background, socioeconomic status, previous academic qualifications, changes in social background characteristics, etc.

Previous academic qualifications

Kasáčová (1996 p. 316) compared the motivation of two groups of TE students according to the type of secondary schools from where they graduated (grammar schools and secondary vocational teacher training schools). The former group showed higher interest in educational and psychological theory. The latter group showed higher interest in the methodology of teaching specific subjects and in actual teaching at schools. They had a better overview of the literature and were better prepared for studies than the graduates from the grammar schools.

In her later study, Kasáčová (2004) showed that the group of primary teachers consisted of 52% graduates from grammar schools, 23% from secondary teacher training vocational schools and 15% from other vocational schools. This ratio changed slightly through years. In the case of pre-primary and primary schools, teachers more often came from secondary teacher training vocational schools. In 2011, this ratio among future science teachers was 83.7 : 12.7 : 3.3 % (Hrubišková & Višváder, 2011).

In her research, Kariková (2000) tested the myth about lower number of talented people among students of TE compared to other study programmes. Her comparison of a sample of future teachers and of future economists showed no statistically significant differences between the cognitive and creative abilities of these two group. Kariková (2010) also showed that for 23% of the respondents in 1974 the choice of the teaching profession was inspired by 'lack of any other study opportunities', whereas in 2009 only 10.4% of them agreed with that.

Socioeconomic background of TE students

Gavora (2002) in his qualitative analysis of life stories of 11 teachers, showed that the decision to become a teacher was usually formed very early, even in the primary years. It emerged gradually in these phases: primary inspiration by the profession, preconception of a teacher's role, identification with the teacher role, primary vision of the profession, elaboration of the vision as the result of experiences, and the final decision to become a teacher. Gavora summarized the most influential factors on choosing a teaching career: socially cohesive family environment in childhood leading to showing an interest in other people; certain personality features, e.g. the sociability, self-confidence, self-promotion, steadiness, reliability, accuracy, responsibility, diligence; experience from one's own schooling period (activities and norms); role pattern – particular teachers; key persons – positive or negative examples; and life crises.

From a psychological research later on in 2004 (Kariková, pp. 54–51), the influence of the tradition of the teaching profession in the family was not confirmed; it seemed the least decisive influence from all motives. The decisive motive was the opportunity to work with children.

Hrubišková & Višváder (2011) researched the socio-economic background of science TE students; 27% of them had a teacher in the family. About 1/2 of the parents were secondary school graduates, 1/3 of them were university graduates. The most educated were mothers of students not planning to become teachers. Those who did not plan to start teaching had 1.32 siblings on average. Those who wanted to become teachers had 1.57 siblings on average; there were fewer students who were only children and more of those who had 3–4 siblings.

As Kariková compared in 2010, in 1974 about 63% of teachers decided for this profession based 'on the influence of other people' and in 2009, it was only 45.6% of the group. This can be explained by higher status of a teaching profession, more extensive influence of parents and of one's own teachers – ideal models, and also by the smaller number of study fields in 1974.

According to several research studies, the decision to study at TE institution was partially influenced by a good example of teachers in the family. Obviously, the responses depended on the type of questions in the investigations. Porubská (1994) found out 43%, Kasáčová (1995, 1996) 15.4%, Kariková (2004) 15%, and Višváder & Hrubišková (2011) 27% respondents who due to the model of their teacher parent were more attracted to the teaching profession.

The influence of other teachers upon TE students' decisions was recognized by 8.5 % of respondents in research by Kasáčová (1995); it was also mentioned in teachers' reproduction of their life stories (Gavora, 2001 & 2002). Concerning the religious background, 81.16 % of respondents were members of Christian churches, and 12.32 % were non-confessional. This difference was even bigger in the group of TE students who planned to become teachers (Hrubišková & Višváder, 2011).

4.1.3 Personal motives and formation of attitudes

In 1994 Schnitzerová investigated a gradual change of attitudes of TE students toward the teaching profession. The first year students described them by positive cognitive statements. Gradually the attitudes became less positive. Last year students used more emotional statements about children, saying, for example, that they would assess children only according to what the pupils knew and not according to his/her effort put into it. They often considered the effort paid to the under-average pupils as unrewarding labor.

Similarly Kasáčová (1996) compared the personal interest in the teaching profession between a group of second grade TE students and a group of third grade students. She found out that the personal attraction of having a chance to work with children dropped from 55% to 36% while the number of students who did not plan to teach after graduation rose.

Another comparison was carried out by Kariková (2004) between TE students and in-service teacher. She found out statistically important differences between their motives for choosing TE and the worries from the beginning of their teaching performance. TE students did not feel prepared to communicate with parents, solve various school situations or do the administrative work. Teachers seemed to be more motivated; able to explain the reason for choosing the profession (meaningful creative job, allowing continuous self-development); expressing fewer worries about communication with parents and finances; more satisfied with the profession; considering their job to be more stable and school climate more positively; more interested in the work itself and evaluating its social meaning more highly; considering pupils to be significantly better and more obedient; more positively evaluating the school management; more objective, rational, closed and reserved. Their negative attitudes expressed in connection with new technology and university TE (not practical enough – e.g. work with SEN children).

In 2006, Valicová found out statistically important differences between the educational motives of a group of respondents for whom the teaching profession was the primary choice (81%) and the alternative choice (19%). About 96% of the first group agreed with the statement "I like to work with the children" as being the most important value. Out of the second group with teaching as an alternative, only 69% believed that it should be the first value; for the rest it was not an important value.

The second motive, "I want to educate somebody", was evidently one of the most important motive in 62% of the first group. Only 38% of the second group considered it as one of the most important motives.

According to a research in 2011 (Hrubišková & Višváder), 45.6 % of TE science students had a strong desire to become teachers; 28.3 % studied TE as an alternative program. Their prior desire was to study at another school (medicine, pharmacy); some of them wanted to reapply to their preferred study program; 13% of them chose TE because of the easy admission (no entrance exam).

4.1.4 Willingness to enter teaching profession and teachers' stamina

According to Eurydice statistics, Slovakia belongs to the group of countries (Finland, Greece, Poland, Portugal, Romania, Spain and UK) where the retention of teachers appears problematic. There is a high percentage of TE graduates who do not actually teach, which may be due to various already mentioned sources of dissatisfaction. Unfortunately, the total amount of money wasted has not been quantified (Černotová & al., 2006) yet.

In the above described comparative study by Kariková (2010), respondents in 1974 considered their choice of a teaching job as final; only up to 14% – in the case of grammar schools – and 2–6% of teachers from other schools would have chosen a different job. In 2009 almost 30% of respondents stated that they would have chosen a different field if given the chance.

In 2011, half of the TE science students group wanted to become teachers after graduation, ¼ of them had not decided yet and ¼ did not plan to become teachers (Hrubišková & Višváder).

Chart 18: Ageing of teachers in Slovakia

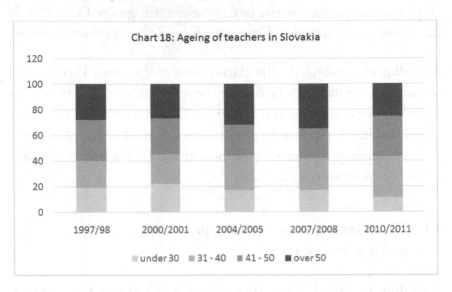

The tendency not to enter the teaching profession after graduation can be seen from Chart 18 on the evident ageing of teachers in Slovakia. Though the recent estimations of *Education by Glance 2013* have showed some stabilization of the number of teachers between and under 40 years old, the number of young teachers is falling down. On one hand a certain group of TE graduates get employed in more attractive jobs with better social conditions, more opportunities to travel and, study languages. On the other side, it is the result of non-conceptual human resources policy; socially unappreciated value of teacher's work; and hard working conditions.

The biggest level of commitment to entry into the teaching profession and the highest level of stamina is observed with female primary TE students/teachers who come from rural areas and smaller towns and those whose parent/parents are teachers (Kasáčová, 2004, p. 45). TE graduates considered the first year in a teaching position to be the most difficult as they faced situations they had not expected. They did not feel to be well prepared by TE institutions to communicate with parents, to advise them, or to work with SEN children (Kasáčová, 1998).

According to current data collected via a website forum (Boledovič, 2013) for parents, students and teachers in 2012, a majority (58%) of young teachers under 30 years old consider leaving their job if the financial situation of their profession does not change. In the group of teachers of 31 – 40 years old, 36% consider leaving; in the group of 41–50 years old, only 20% consider leaving while about 33% teachers over 50 years old consider leaving.

To sum up, the number of TE students/teachers who would choose another job was at first growing – from 14% in 1974 to 24% in 1998 and 33% in 2004. Then it started to stabilize by 30% in 2009%; 25% not decided yet and 25% not planning to teach in 2011; to about 30% in 2013.

4.1.5 Qualitative research of teachers' recruitment

Having a teacher educator's access to personally talk to and observe TE students during their studies, we decided to accomplish our own investigation of determinants of their decision to become a teacher. The research questions were: Why do young people study at TE institutions nowadays? What influenced them to study TE? What do they think about the demands of the teaching profession and their own stamina for accomplishing it?

The research by Hanesová (2013) was completed via interviews about their opinions and segments of life stories connected with the teaching profession. A Guided memory recalling of one's own specific experience in order to reflect one's motivation and decision making was carried out. The respondents also had to compare it with those of their TE colleagues, and thus to indicate the reasons for remaining in the teaching profession. Thus the occurrence of any responses was feasible. The aim was to collect and soft data in order to bring to light the current variety of categories taking part in current recruitment, and which, if desired, might be used for quantitative research in the future. The quantitative weight of several responses seemed interesting too and worthy of mentioning. After analyzing the data, the comparison with the previous research was done. We expected that the range of motivational factors of the current TE students would be wider than those of the previous generations. At the same time, some of the motivational factors, such as an influence of having a teacher in the family or interest in working with children or teaching, were presupposed to be factors with a strong stability index. Due to the choice of the qualitative character of the research, the sample was relatively small. It consisted of 53 Slovak respondents (22 TE students, 26 teachers and 5 TE graduates); and 9 Czech 9 TE students. Only 6.4% of the sample were men which reminds the current feminized situation in lower education both in Slovakia and Czech Republic.

Analysis, interpretation and discussion of the collected data

As it was mentioned above, the respondents were not given a list of choices. It can be assumed that their responses reflect the strongest influence, not exhaustively all objective effects.

Most homogenous group of Slovak respondents (30%) described the decision for a teaching profession as a ***spontaneous childhood decision***. It is a decrease of more than 15% comparing to the previous research: 51.4% of TE students in 1994 (Porubská) and 44.6% of them in 1995 (Kasáčová) developed their positive attitude toward the teaching profession in their childhood.

More than 1/4 of the respondents radically rejected any correlation between their ***socio-economic background*** and their decision to study TE. Several respondents mentioned that in villages and small towns the profession of teachers was more valued than in bigger habitats. In one case, 70% of students in her study group were from villages, with one being from a village with a typical Roma settlement. But generally, the respondents think that the decision of young people to study at TE is more due to their personal characteristics than to their childhood background. Among their schoolmates, they did not recognize any pattern concerning the background that would be characteristic just for teachers. They think that there are many combinations of factors influencing this decision and that it is not possible to generalize any strong connection between coming from village/town/city, being more or less or none at all religiously active. They argument is that there are plenty of young people with similar backgrounds around them, and yet they are not willing to be teachers, but they become businesspeople, lawyers or politicians. It depends mainly on their view of life meaning.

One respondent explained that the future teachers' parents are predominantly either teachers or secondary school graduates (workers, farmers, etc.). There are a few from a medical doctor's family. But a TE student from a manager or lawyer's family is a very unusual phenomenon. Another respondent commented that in the past there was a visible connection between the teacher's background and his/her decision to become a teacher. But at present the quality of education has fallen down so drastically that even those people who are not suitable for this profession apply for the job, and so it is hard to say what teacher background that is.

Concerning **religious background**, 42% of respondents said they personally had a Christian worldview but they were not aware of the influence of religion on their schoolmates.

We found out that all Slovak respondents who were willing and able to participate in the inquiry had a personally positively attitude toward the teaching profession. Here are **the reasons why the respondents chose TE/teaching profession**:

Half of the respondents *praise **the 'beauty' of the teaching profession***. A similar percentage of respondents were attracted to work with children, taking care of them and organizing them was found out in the mentioned research in 1995 and 2008. All of our respondents showed genuine interest to become a teacher and praised the teaching profession. It is the fulfillment of their childhood dream; their life mission/calling (for 3 respondents – a calling from God), and a natural decision for a meaningful, satisfactory profession which can change the conditions of children from socially deprived areas. To be a teacher means to love teaching and having an influence upon people's lives. Almost half of the respondents considered positive attitudes to children to be cause of their studying TE/being a teacher. For 20% of them, the teaching profession is the actualization of their natural ability, talent, hobby, love to work with people, need to communicate or to manage people. E.g., "I literally cannot do anything else than teaching." "I love playing the role of a teacher."

One third of respondents indicated the ***influence of another person*** on their decision. They were influenced by observing their teachers' work and attitudes (10%); by learning to help educate younger siblings and other children, to understand their needs (17%); by teachers in the family – parents, grandparents, and uncles (10%); and by other ways of encouragement.

The influential teachers in the childhood became a source of knowledge combined with positive attitudes and deep personal relationships toward children, expertise, love of their subject, willingness to share their experiences and to reveal its meaning and beauty.

A few respondents commented that though having a teacher in the family can trigger the decision to study TE, but only up to 50%. The demotivating 50% is caused by the persistent problems in education. Sometimes teachers in the family even decide to discourage their offspring so that not to choose the teaching profession, mainly because of economic reasons, wishing that their children would have a better paid and higher socially esteemed profession.

One special comment confirmed positive influence on becoming teacher of those family members who could not teach under communism because of their religious worldview.

Personal growth and self-realization was the reason for becoming a teacher for one third of respondents. They think teaching is a creative dynamic profession with no chance for stagnation (10%). It is a prestigious job bringing adventure, friends, a right to manage (9%); giving a chance for personal change, growth (e.g. in patience, overcoming personal weaknesses (9%), a good opportunity to learn from others, enjoyment in the teaching process; fulfillment of love to study or an interest in the subjects themselves (13%). It is a good combination how to fulfill one's love to some subjects and to teaching (2).

Some respondents mentioned also the ***utilitarian advantages of teaching profession:*** a comfortable job with enough free time, vacations, good working hours, suitable for perspective mothers, easy recyclable preparations, etc. (10%). Some respondents commented on the insufficiently financially rewarding profession.

There were also ***other reasons for studying TE***, e.g. to learn how to bring up one's own children (10%), to help one's own child with special education needs; to fulfill one's philanthropic desires; to continue in previous studies on education; or even to have fun in life.

Similarly to the amount of previous mentioned studies (1995, 2000, 2004, 2006, 2011), for 18% of schoolmates of our respondents TE was only ***the second choice***, an opportunity to be admitted to a university study with none or easy entrance exams, one of the ways to get a Master's degree in an easier way; a good chance to study at a university and have a chance to teach too. ("And in the end teaching is OK or even interesting" (15%); a bridge between secondary school and becoming a researcher – an open door for PhD studies/teaching at the university; a way to get to other more desired jobs (IT at school); a stable job with a stable income.

Though only 2 respondents did not want to teach themselves, they estimated that only up to 30% from their schoolmates plan to teach after graduation. This estimation is twice smaller than those from previous research and it was influenced by the fact that it was only an opinion about others. The reasons for not teaching after graduation include: either lack of teaching opportunities, or continuation in PhD studies, going abroad to improve one's language competence, finding employment in other fields or in private businesses. One student would like to become a school inspector.

According to 1/6 of respondents the present situation differs from the past in a lower status of teachers. The previous generations used to honor the teaching profession and so they led their children to respect the teachers. Now the parents doubt the expertise of the teachers, "excuse their children from school for no real reasons", "allow them too many things", etc. The disrespectful behavior of students, their aversion to learning and the low financial reward are the main hindrances for young TE students to enter their profession. Several TE students are afraid of entering a job as they are not satisfied with the level of practical preparation at TE institutions and they do not feel competent to start teaching. TE offers too much theory and little practical application.

Similar to the Slovak responses, all **Czech respondents** expressed a *positive attitude* toward the teaching profession. They consider it to be a *fulfillment of a personal dream* since childhood/a personal calling; a result of a courageous or naïve decision; preference for this type of work; a job with relative stability; a creative job; fulfillment of desire to study, to work with children and to gain experience with educational work.

On the other hand, for many students TE studies are just an *alternative chance* to get another degree and better payment. It takes care of their need of a MA qualification. Entrance exams might be as easy as the study itself is.

Several Czech respondents mentioned the *utilitarian advantages* of a teaching profession, such as good working hours and vacation, stability, and finances. Only a third of respondents considered choosing TE profession as the means of fulfilling one's love of the study of the subjects and of continuous growth. Half of the respondents thought that the *socio-economic background* had an influence on their decision to become a teacher. A few were influenced by opportunities to help with children' upbringing.

The Czech group consisted of people with assorted motivation ranging from those who wanted to become teachers as the first choice to those who did not want to become teachers but later started to be content with this study.

4.2 Research on feminization of teachers

Feminization – denoting a predominant number of female teachers over male teachers – is generally viewed as one of the outward signs of the crisis in or degradation of the teaching profession. According to Cviková & Filadelfiová (2008, p. 40), the critical number for declaring feminization is when the number of female teachers crosses the 60% threshold. Statistical data from the vast majority of otherwise highly developed school systems (with the exception of tertiary level) throughout the world show that the number of women in the teaching profession is far higher than 60% (up to 99100% in pre-primary education).

In Western societies this 'crisis of the primary teaching profession' reached a peak in the last decade of the 20th century (Kosová, 2010, p. 38). Recent data show that though there was a slight decrease in the number of females in education around the year 2000, a few years ago the increase in the number of females in teaching again reached the 60% threshold (according to UNESCO websites).

On the other hand, some researchers have suggested that the higher number of males in the teaching profession was usually the case in less developed countries (Kasáčová & Tabačáková, 2010, p. 112). This suggestion could lead to the following questions: What do the numbers of female or male teachers actually mean for the quality of education and its results? Is the prevalence of female teachers always a negative sign? What are the actual reasons for the higher number of males in less developed countries? Do they indicate any plausible patterns to be implemented in countries with high feminization? According to Neugebauer at all, "teaching is a female sex-segregated profession in literally all advanced societies, while it is male dominated in developing countries (most visibly in African countries). In the latter countries, women do not obtain higher education and are consequently not able to work as teachers – thus the share of female teachers is low. In addition, recent research has shown that, once the level of female tertiary enrollment begins to rise in a given country, having a higher percentage of women in female sex-segregated academic professions is an almost automatic consequence, as long as female preferences for traditionally female occupations do not change."(Neugebauer et al, 2010, p. 1).

4.2.1 Motives of males and females deciding on a teaching career

Besides statistical data on feminization, there has been a lot of effort put into investigations of the factors leading to feminization in Slovakia (and partially in the Czech Republic) especially by searching motives for studying/entering the teaching profession. Not only in Slovakia, but also in the Czech Republic the dominant proportion of women is an undeniable statistical fact (Gőbelová, 2009).

Already in 1974, Špendla, in his research of teachers' motives for choosing a teaching career, found that the most important motive was respondents' love for children, and a desire to work in a child-centred environment. His participants' responses explicitly showed that teaching was considered to be a job suitable for women. The desire to educate emerged as the second most important motive.

The biggest category of responses in most research studies about these motives was the desire to work with and teach children, a decision often made in childhood (15% in Porubská, 1994, 51.4% in Kasáčová, 1995, 2002, 2004). According to Gavora (2001, 2002) the most important factors were the family environment during childhood; then personality features of the students; experiences from own schooling; role models; key people; and life crises.

In 2009, a Slovak psychologist, Kariková repeated Špendla's research from 1974 with her group of education students. While researching their spontaneity in deciding to enter the teaching profession, as well as some positive and negative aspects of the teaching profession, she confirmed rising levels of feminization, the declining status of the teaching profession, and growing pressure on teachers from negative features of the teaching profession. She compared the proportion of female teachers in 2009 with that of 1974. It appeared to be 10% higher in 2009, confirming the growing trend of feminization in education. Analysis of respondents' answers showed stronger inclination of females to choose the teaching profession. In connection with these data, an interesting finding emerged from Kryštoň's research (1994) into the opinions of upper secondary school students and their decision to study teacher education. Kryštoň's participants considered teaching to be the third most attractive profession – not only by females (54%) but also by 39% male students.

Kariková (2005) researched several angles of feminization in the teaching profession, e.g. initial motivation, adaptation, performance, stamina, typical signs of primary teacher's personality (1994, 2004, and 2005). She found out that the male respondents, especially those who were married or going to get married, did not plan to start a teaching career but wanted to find a more profitable job. The fact that the groups of future primary teachers at Faculties of Education in Slovakia have consisted almost entirely of female students was reflected also in several research studies on teachers in Slovakia.

The highest commitment to start teaching and to persevere in teaching was reported by females coming from rural areas and smaller towns whose parent was a teacher (Kasáčová, 2004). Similar results were revealed by a Czech researcher (Havlík, 1995) showing that the male teacher education students in his group were also less motivated to start teaching after graduation.

In her overview of other research studies on motives for applying into teacher education in Slovakia (and the Czech Republic) and especially in her own investigation in 2013/14, Hanesová (2014) described the prevalent desire to study teaching education as expressed as an answer to an open question "Why did you choose to study in this study program?". Almost 50% of the respondents (100% females) decided for *the teaching profession* because they considered it a "beautiful, meaningful, satisfactory profession ... Similar number of respondents were attracted to work with children, take care of them and organize them ... For them, teaching had been a fulfillment of their childhood dream, their life mission, a natural decision with a potential to change the conditions of children from socially deprived areas. Their desire to be a teacher grew out of their love of teaching and a chance of having an influence upon people's lives. Almost half of the respondents considered positive attitudes to children to be the cause of their studying TE/being a teacher. Another group (up to 20%) decided to study teaching because of the potential for actualization of their natural ability, talent, hobby, love of working with people, and desire to communicate or to manage people."

Another important data from Hanesová's research (2014) was that one third of respondents decided for this profession as a direct influence of *another person/s:* observing their own teachers (10%); helping younger siblings and other children (17%); having teachers in the family – parents, grandparents, uncles and aunts (10%). One third of the respondents valued the potential of personal growth and self-realization in the teaching profession as they considered it to be "a creative dynamic profession bringing adventure, friends, a right to manage, potential for personal change and growth, a good opportunity to learn from others, enjoyment in the teaching process; fulfilment of love to study or an interest in the subjects themselves (13%). It is a good combination of how to fulfil one's love to some subjects and to teaching." About 10% of Hanesová's respondents also mentioned "the utilitarian advantages of the teaching profession: a comfortable job with enough free time, vacations, good working hours, suitable for perspective mothers, easy recyclable preparations", though others commented on the fact that teaching is an insufficiently financially rewarding profession.

4.2.2 Other research on teachers from the gender point of view

In 2008, an interesting publication about research ASPECT in *Gender issues 2008* in education in four countries (the Czech Republic, Poland, Slovak Republic and Ukraine) was published:

- The *Czech* researchers found out that in 2008, the gender distribution of students at college-type of upper secondary education (so called grammar schools) and other secondary schools matched the gender distribution of teachers at those feminized schools. Male teachers were more often employed in technical and vocational schools. "Work in education sector is less financially attractive in general, but, even here, women earn less than men" (Ciprová et al., 2008, pp. 18 & 36). According to the opinions of respondents, female teachers teaching at elementary school were "likely to become associated with women ... being seen as a job suitable for women rather than for men, connected with raising children and the transferal of the cultural patterns traditionally ascribed to women." In 2008 the Czech school was "a gender-segregated space leading to reproduction of gender stereotypes".
- The *Polish* researchers Dzierzgowska and Rutkowska (2008, p. 74) described the Polish school system in 2008 as a pyramid at the base of which there was the biggest number of women (kindergarten and primary teachers). The higher the educational

level, the smaller numbers of teachers. "At the top (academic) level there are the fewest women".

- The *Ukrainian* study by Kisselyova & Musiyenko (2008) reported that the education system in Ukraine in 2008 was feminized and gender-insensitive (with 98.67% of women in pre-primary education).

- According to the views of the *Slovak* reporters (Cviková & Filadelfiová, 2008, p. 119), teachers were "the key risk factor in fostering gender equality in the heavily feminized education system". The teaching profession seemed to "reinforce the stereotypical gender division of labor". As research ASPEKT (2008) – and others (Hanesová, 2014) – showed teachers themselves have regarded the working arrangements and conditions of the teaching profession to be real advantages of this profession. Thus, they expressed their preference to spend more time in their homes with their own children than in professional development. This and other issues (for example, that female teachers do not consider themselves but their husbands to the breadwinners) indicate that "the gender bias in the teaching profession reinforces gender stereotypes of teachers – in relation to themselves and to their students" (Cviková &Filadelfiová, 2008, p. 118).

A different but interesting view on the choice of the teaching profession by male and female applicants was presented by a Slovak expert Čižmáriková (2015). In her research study, Čižmáriková provided insight into issues of value orientation of teacher education (TE) students in Ethics Education. She compared male and female preferences and found interesting differences between these two groups that may help show why fewer males than females apply for the teaching profession. While female TE students attributed the highest significance to the value of self-transcendence, male students ascribed the greatest importance to the value of stimulation, self-determination and hedonism, which are values belonging to the category 'openness to change'. Women especially, underlined the quality of interpersonal relationships and harmonious relationships to the world, peace, tolerance, the welfare of others, caring, honesty, loyalty, forgiveness and responsibility. In contrast, male students prefer exciting challenges, change, movement in life, adventure and to some extent risk. The value of hedonism was assigned by males as the second most important value, together with the value of self-determination. Females placed hedonism to the 6th rung along with the value of success. To sum up, for male TE students the statistically most significant values are self-determination, hedonism, security, benevolence, universalism, achievement. The second group of values consisted of the values of tradition and power. Female TE students formed three groups of statistically significant values. For them the most important values in life were benevolence, universalism, self-determination and safety.

4.2.3 Discussion on feminization in schools based on research

Feminization in education is not a new phenomenon in European or North American society, but it has long historical roots. Lather (1987) and Grumet (1995) studied the status of the teaching profession "as an extension of domestic labor". According to Grumet&McCoy (1988 in 2000), "feminization of teaching took place around the time of the Industrial Revolution, the practice of hiring women to replace the man who had been the school masters (but who were leaving the villages for employment in the cities) was rationalized with a sentimental celebration of women's maternal gifts … Women were praised for the self-sacrifice and for their modesty and these features were considered to be traits of the proper teachers" (p. 431). According to Neugebauer et al. (2010, p. 1), "in the United States … the teaching profession became a predominantly female profession as early as in the late 19th century, initial efforts to recruit more men into teaching were made between the two world wars." The primary reason for doing so was to avoid the "feminization of boys, who would be less able to develop their masculinity without appropriate role models" during their schooling.

Since then scholars have engaged in extensive discussions and research on the issue of feminization in education in their effort to comprehend its reasons, to explain it and to make twofold suggestions – either how to raise the social status of the teaching profession and thus more successfully recruit men into the lower educational levels or how to arrange better working conditions for more women to teach at the tertiary level – in the universities. For example, researchers Mistry & Sood (2013) from Nottingham Trent University decided to investigate the stereotypical opinion that working with young children is a "woman's profession". They found out that men were being put off working in primary schools because of negative stereotypes "combined with fears that they would be falsely labelled as pedophiles", though according to research the same men in the research by Nottingham Trent and Bedfordshire universities were confident to work with young children (Paton, 2013): A "number of studies have shown that males find teaching unattractive or to be too female friendly or that their maleness always attracts attention from others or the focus is on males as role models (Skelton 2007; Brownhill 2010). But there are very few studies to substantiate these assertions for males entering the EY sector".

Gender segregation as an issue in choosing a career was also an object of research supported by the Slovak research APVV Agency, carried out by Jesenková (2008), based on several studies, e.g. by Czech sociologist Čermáková. Using historical examples, she stated that when a profession was quite accessible to women, the impression was given "that it was an easy job or that lower professional preparation was needed", which resulted in "dropping down the financial rewards as well as the social status of that profession". So "feminization of schooling seemingly appears to be one of the reasons of de-professionalization of the teaching profession" (p. 3).

Slovak authors Cviková and Filadelfiová (2008) completed research called "ruzovyamodrysvet.sk" (pingandblueworld) on gender issues (called *Gender Sensitisation in the Educational Process at Elementary and Secondary Schools as Preparation for Future Job Desegregation* Programme of the European EQUAL Community Initiative, in cooperation with the Institute for Public Affairs and the FOCUS agency, Aspekt) in Slovakia. They pointed to the danger of such perceptions of the problems in the school system, saying that the quantitative feminization itself – the rising number of women working in schools – was not the main problem. According to them, the main issue is the gender hierarchy in rewarding one's work. Therefore they suggest that researchers focus more on the fact of "disadvantaging and belittling women instead of simply identifying feminization as the problem" (Cviková & Filadelfiová, 2008, p. 3).

Neugebauer et al. (2010) also connect feminization with the need of self-realization, free choice of one's career. They argue that "the current share of female teachers at school may be deduced from women's educational opportunities in past decades and their opportunities of participating in the labor market today. In sum, the gender of the teacher is not relevant for the increasing educational success of girls. Rather, equal gender opportunities in a given country encourage girls to realize their academic potential, while at the same time making it more likely for women to become teachers" (p. 1).

It appears that the discussions and polemics about the imbalance of females and males in education have uncovered several unsolved issues, e.g.:

- Reasons for the low social status of teachers and the low prestige of the teaching profession; overlooking the work of teachers by society and not comprehending the burden of work of the teachers by society; feminization as one of the reasons of low professional self-awareness and of lower social appreciation; more women working at the lower levels of education, often in more demanding socially disadvantaged areas with lower salaries;
- Gender stereotypes about the relative social status of female and male teachers as hidden curricula in schools – the attitudes

and the behavior of teachers to boys and girls may be a source of their attitude toward teaching profession (Neugebauer et al., 2010)[2];

- Agreement/disagreement with the traditional opinion that the man is the breadwinner of the family and so the low wages (far below the national income average) of teachers prevent men from entering and staying in the teaching profession. It was a research focus of the European EQUAL Community Initiative funded by the European Social Fund, initiated by ASPEKT and conducted by the Institute for Public Affairs and FOCUS in the years 2005 – 2008. Its findings carried out as part of the project ruzovyamodrysvet.sk (pinkandblueworld.sk) – Gender Sensitization in the Educational Process at Elementary and Secondary Schools as Preparation for Future Job Desegregation described by Filadelfiová (2008);

- Opinion that the teaching profession is particularly suitable for women due to the organization of working time facilitating the 'juggling family and professional life' of the family and professional life – thus a lot of "female teachers do not perceive gender inequalities in their profession";

- The inner dynamics inside the teaching staff in one school – female school principals are often hesitant to accept male teachers because they fear losing their position due to the presence of the man.

---

[2] The authors examined whether teacher gender in fact had an impact on the academic achievement of male and female students. They questioned the hypothesis about feminization causing the potential lack of role models for boys and then subsequently in fewer male applicants for teaching profession. Also they investigated next hypothesis that the growing "feminization" of the teaching profession might explain the educational disadvantages for boys and the success of girls in schools. The authors challenge this argumentation by saying that there was a need to ask how cross-country differences regarding the percentage of female teachers came about in the first place, and why the total share of female teachers has risen over the past decades (p. 20).

As these points have indicated, feminization does not have a straightforward solution; it is a complex societal issue. For instance, observing the realistic and positive approach of how, for example, Finland raised the social status of teachers and how it treats feminization might be encouraging for other countries as well. Our suggestion is that this phenomenon should be studied more thoroughly and diligently from several angles. The potential changes must be implemented patiently, in ways that are sensitive to local historical developments in education, and that make every effort to meet the individual age, gender and needs of pupils, students and teachers. Some researchers, for example, have recommended that male teacher education students should be encouraged to undertake work placements in primary schools – under the leadership of an existing male head teacher – to give them a positive experience of working with young children. Generalizations or stereotypes do not help; deep scientific analysis and evaluation, and then persuasion and good modeling might be a successful way forward.

Previous research in Slovakia showed that the main motivating factors influencing the decision to become a teacher were: family influence, the influence of the teachers that the students have met during their life, school experience, the influence of peers and altruistic motivations. Problems of teachers' stamina, willingness to stay in the profession after the studies have proved to be connected with students' expectations from the teaching studies; changes in their attitudes influenced by the studies; personality preconditions for the performance of the profession; one' willingness to work as a teacher after completion of the studies; forming one's professional identity, and developing student's reflexivity during preparation for the job and building one's teaching capabilities.

As our predominantly qualitative investigation showed, TE students can be divided into four groups according to the motives of why they study at a TE institution:

- *From psychological reasons*: They want to become teachers, though they might have a naïve idea of what it means. They loved to play the role of a teacher in their childhood or they had good experiences working with children. Besides those who dream, some really want to teach, some just want to study. Their decision was often influenced by other teachers, work with children, their love toward the specific subject etc.;

- *From personal reasons*: They enjoy learning opportunities and chances to grow personally in many areas; they want to become professional in parenthood;
- *From pragmatic reasons:* This group – mostly women – think that teaching does not require a lot of effort, and so it would be a suitable job in a time when they themselves have small children and need to work. A few TE students think TE is an easy (maybe the easiest) university study, so will be the job;
- *From other reasons:* They might not be sure yet about their future career or say, "Let me try teaching and then I will see."

Those for whom becoming a teacher after graduation is the first choice, display some, if not all of the following characteristics: They **love children** and want to influence children's lives; in their opinion teaching has of high value, aspirations and ideals. They **love to learn**; to study themselves; they love the content of the subjects. They have a **desire to teach others**, to share with their expertise. They **believe in the results** of good education/knowledge, moral character and other results of education. Of course, some TE students only want to **get a university degree** (B.A. or M.Ed.). They either do not have any clear ambitions about their future yet or they consider TE study as an alternative, maybe leading to another profession, research, etc.

Being a teacher is a unique profession. As one of our respondents put it: "Teaching is the most frequent job that we as children have observed and practiced since our childhood. So I decided to study TE somehow subconsciously and automatically after having observed my teachers at primary and secondary school for years. I kept thinking: What will I do in such a situation? Not: What might I do? I always had my ideal teachers, and so my steps toward this decision were sure and automatic."

4.3 Professiographic research on teacher's activities

One of the most recent analysis and evaluation of teacher's activities has been the research project *The Profession of Pre-primary Teacher and Primary Teacher within a Dynamic Concept*, carried out by three Central European Faculties of Teacher Education in the years 2008 – 2010, with the support of the Slovak Research and Development Agency (APVV-0026-07). The purpose of the research was to identify specific professional activities of pre-primary and primary teachers, to reveal their structure and the time ratio between them. Its importance was in the fact that it succeeded in uncovering important data on the teaching profession.

4.3.1 Research sample

The **research sample** of pre-primary (kindergarten) teachers consisted 641 teachers – 43.53% from Slovakia, 33.39% from the Czech Republic and 25.4% from Poland (Kasáčová, 2011, pp. 137-154). The sample of primary teachers consisted of 437 teachers – 51.25 % from Slovakia, 23.34% from the Czech Republic and 25.4% from Poland. For the purposes of the research, these teachers recorded 4670 working days and 1572 weekend days in total.

4.3.2 Research methodology

Thus the main methods of professiography used in this research were questionnaires, observation, interviews and especially recording sheets (Babiaková, 2012, pp. 222–242) During three different seasons (spring – autumn – winter), always for a duration of two weeks, the teachers were asked to monitor all their own professional activities minutely (starting at 7:00 – 16:00 on a working day, but also after 16:00 and during weekends) and fill them in the following professiographic record (Appendix No. 1) (Kasáčová, 2011, pp. 83–99).

After the pre-research stage, the researchers succeeded in preparing a profile structure of professional activities of teachers at both pre-primary (ISCED 0) and primary (ISCED 1) levels. The piloting in-service teachers identified almost 30 activities that determine their profession (Appendix No. 2 and 3).

The main emphasis of the research was on finding out the real **workload of teachers** as well as the (time) **structure of activities** performed by teachers during their working days and weekends.

4.3.3 Research results

Pre-primary teachers

The research showed that the highest number of hours per week (Monday – Sunday) spent in professional activities by pre-primary teachers was 58.3 hours in the Czech Republic (due to "school in nature" – 1–2 weeks spent with children off-school in the countryside – as partially indicated by Burkovičová et al, 2011, p. 241), 42.20 hours in Slovakia and 37.97 hours in Poland (Babiaková et al, 2011, p. 132).

As the final comparative study shows, some differences in the duration of respective professional activities recorded by the research participants reflected specifics of the countries. *Czech* pre-primary teachers – respondents in the research sample – spent more time on a) planning the educational activities; b) setting the educational environment and organizing the educational activities; c) motivating students; d) solving conflicts and tensions during the educational process, etc. The activity on which the Czech and Slovak teachers spent most time was teaching itself as well as managing the educational activities inside the kindergarten. *Polish* pre-primary teachers' main activity was preparing and creating teaching aids. *Slovak* teachers invested quite a lot of their working time in participation in various committees and school bodies as well as organizing and managing a school club according to the interests of children/requirements of parents.

Another difference among the countries was the season when the workload of the teachers was most intensive (depending on various activities that the teachers were involved in). In Slovakia, the most intensive season for pre-primary teachers was in the spring, in the Czech Republic in the autumn. Polish teachers did not record differences in seasons.

The research revealed some interesting data not only about the regular activities, but also the irregular activities of pre-primary teachers. The Slovak teachers mentioned the following:

- Administrative work (inventory of furniture);
- Activities connected with various festivals (Teachers' Day, Mother's Day, Children's Day);
- Decorating the school or classrooms after renovations/painting the walls;
- Buying new teaching materials;
- Buying toys, rewards for children;
- Visiting various cultural events or organizations;
- Organizing performances for various groups of community;
- 'School in nature' week/weeks;
- Skiing or swimming training;
- School projects;
- Writing school curriculum;
- Class trips;
- Discussions with policemen, firemen, and other professions;
- Taking photos of the whole class;
- Activities preparing preschoolers for their school attendance.

Primary teachers

The average amount of time spent in the performance by primary teachers in the research sample during the working hours, but also after 4 p. m. and during the weekend, in Poland was 39.62 hours, in Slovakia

43.07 hours and in the Czech Republic 46.56 hours (Babiaková, 2012, p. 232).

It is useful to compare these data with older research studies. According to a study in 2000 (Blížkovský et al, p. 251), which investigated the workload of teachers in the same three countries (Slovakia, Poland and the Czech Republic), the average workload of all investigated teachers (levels ISCED 1, ISCED 2 and ISCED 3) was 41.8 hours in Slovakia, 42.51 hours in the Czech Republic and 40.4 hours in Poland. That means that during one decade the workload in two countries might have increased (by 1.59 hours in Slovakia and by 4.23 in the Czech Republic).

In all three countries, primary teachers spent the highest amount of time planning lessons and teaching: 24.3 hours in Slovakia, 27 hours in the Czech Republic and 25 hours in Poland, including managing activities and coordinating students' work. The second most time-demanding category of activities included activities aimed at activating and motivating students (Burkovičová et al, 2011, pp. 255–256). This fact reflects the raising trend of students' passivity and challenge for the current teachers.

The average time spent by primary teachers in activities directly connected with teaching and preparation for teaching found in the research is documented in Chart 19.

Chart 19: Time spent in teaching/lesson preparation (in minutes)

Activities of primary teachers directly connected with teaching and lesson preparation during working week	**Slovakia** (minutes)	**Czech Republic** (minutes)	**Poland** (minutes)
Projecting and planning the lessons	176	**223**	132
Checking the preparation of students for the lessons	93	99	61

Activating students, motivating activities	131	130	**182**
Explaining new subject matter	**145**	129	134
Management and coordination of learning activities of students	316	363	365
Testing of learning results	124	131	77
Assessment – in direct contact with pupils	99	105	70
Preparation/teaching individual plans for students with special educational needs	82	64	**171**
Recognizing and solving behavioral situations	80	68	69
Marking and grading students' assignments	111	**161**	110
Creating teaching aids	100	145	131
Together	1 457	1 618	1502

Source: Babiaková, S. Komparácia profesijných činností slovenských, českých a poľských učiteľov na primárnom stupni školy. *Pedagogická orientace,* 2012, Vol. 22, No. 2, p. 236.

The differences between the work loads of primary teachers in various seasons were minimal. Slovak and Czech primary teachers showed the highest level of professional performance in the spring. Polish teachers showed the most balanced workload over the year, although the most active season for them was the winter season (Filipiak et al., 2011, pp. 285–314). The research confirmed that there were differences in the level of work load on different days of the week, with Friday being the least loaded day. In the case of Slovak teachers, a statistically significant difference was found between the work performance on Wednesday and Friday (Babiaková et al, 2011, p. 145). The school timetables tend to plan fewer lessons on Friday, reflecting the potential tiredness of the students after spending the whole week at school.

Research also showed that primary teachers often still use traditional explanatory methods of teaching – verbal instructions, resulting in an imbalance between somewhat over-active teachers and less active students. Learner-centered education has not yet become a reality in primary schools. Czech teachers spent more time preparing lessons and teaching materials than Slovak teachers. As a result of school reforms in Poland, teachers use a lot of pre-prepared worksheets and workbooks; this may be one reason why they spent less time planning and preparing the lessons and teaching aids. Polish teachers spent more time preparing individual plans for students with special educational needs than the other two categories of teachers. Solving problems related to bad behavior took the least amount of time.

Differences among the three countries were also found in the connection between the time spent in professional activities and the length of teaching experience of primary teachers. In the Czech sample, the busiest teachers, spending the most time in their profession during the week, were teachers with 20–30 years of teaching experience, whereas in Poland the unexperienced and in Slovakia the most experienced group of teachers reported the highest work load.

Activities in the last two categories of primary teachers' performance were similar to those mentioned in the case of pre-primary teachers. Teachers spent 6.7% of their average week time in activities belonging to category E. A lot of time had to be devoted to standard activities, such as administrative work, writing students' reports, or rewriting curricula. More time investment was needed also in over-standard professional activities, e.g. preparing students for various Olympiads and other competitions, recycling, and meetings with the community, as well as after-school tutorage (assistance to students working on some assignments). Also, the range of other-than-teaching roles of teachers and the range of membership in various committees and boards was wider than in the case of pre-primary teachers (such as the role of a career consultant for the 14-15 year olds). Of course, primary teachers had to perform several 'non-professional' activities that were often time-consuming, perceived either as useful (recycling, buying new teaching aids, preparing costumes for students' performance), or often as a burden (cleaning the desks, fundraising, checking students' hair for lice, copying materials).

Comparing the data from professiography with questionnaires, it warrants saying that the teachers' questionnaires showed more hours spent in the profession then the actual records by individual teachers (Babiaková, 2012, p. 226). This difference might be rooted in the fact that when teachers have to perform their teaching and observe it at the same time, the data might have been modified to some extent. Similarly, the Swiss researcher, Landert, in his professiographic research (2006), found out that there was only a 20% match between what the teachers wrote in their records and the reality: 37% of teachers recorded higher workload and 43% recorded lower number than the actual figures (Landert, 2006). Researchers aware of this risk in using professiograms prepared a precise triangulated system of methods. They paid attention to the piloting stages of all of them and to editing all instructions for teachers in the research sample.

To sum up the results of the research described above, it is important to say that statistically there were no cardinally significant differences between the three investigated countries. But, of course, there were differences between the structure of professional activities of pre-primary and primary teachers as well as in the time spent carrying them out.

4.3.4 Comparison and discussion on the meaning of research on teachers

Professiographic research has the potential to become a means of painting real pictures of the teacher's profession. It reveals the professional character of teaching. Thus it can become an effective tool in raising its social status and in motivating new applicants to choose teaching as a meaningful, worthwhile life career – similarly to other popular professions as medicine, law, veterinary medicine, and firefighting (e.g. according to Mihály, 2014).

High-quality professiographic research in individual countries or regions is then also an extremely useful means for effective international comparisons, finding similarities and diversities, but especially for reflecting the value and quality of one's own research in the world-wide context. Hanesová (2009, p. 162; 2011, pp. 155–168) – one of the members of the APVV research team – compared the results of her investigations with other available data from previous research on teachers' activities by researchers in other countries (e.g. Fazis, Schmidt & Matas (1994), Forneck & Schriever (2001); Gallen, Karlenzig and Tamney (1995); Galton, McBeath et al (2002); L. Hargreaves, Cunningham, Hansen, McIntyre, Oliver & Pell (2007), Harvey & Spinney (2000); Kane (2008), Landert (2002), Posch (2004), Trachsler, Inversini, Ulich & Wűsler (2003); Troman (1996), Webb, R., Vulliamy, G., Hämäläinen, Sarja, Kimonen & Nevalainen (2004) - more in Appendix No. 5). Being able to look at the results of one's own professiographic research against the background of research in other countries gives real potential for more effective use of one's research results for development either of the theory or practice of teaching.

For example, when speaking about teacher's activities from the point of their work load, it is possible to compare these international resources with the results from the above-described APVV projects and its data on Slovakia, Poland and the Czech Republic and find out the workload of teachers from the comparative perspective. Though there is no space here to describe those studies, it is necessary to say that they usually counted hours spent in teaching, lesson preparation, testing and assessing, producing teaching aids, administrative activities, contacts with teachers/ students/ colleagues and community, other activities (supervision of students after lessons), self-study, etc. Of course, it always depends on the methodology, and most of the research studies reported in the previous Chart No. 19 did not use the same criteria. We present these data in Chart 20 only for orientation:

Chart 20: Work load of teachers

Country/year	Hours
Hong Kong 2006	63.5
Great Britain 2006	50.1
Canada 2004	53.3
Tasmania 2004	48.7
New Zealand 1995	47.35
Australia 2005	47.1
Czech Republic 2010	46.56
Austria 2000	43.44
Slovakia 2010	43
Poland 2010	39.62
Older: Switzerland 1999	38.25

Source: Hanesová, D. Komparatívny pohľad na výskum učiteľa a jeho profesijných činností. In Kasáčová, B., Cabanová, M. (eds.) *Profesia učiteľa v preprimárnej a primárnej edukácii v teórii a praxi*. Banská Bystrica: PF UMB, 2009, p. 162.

Of course the actual reading of 'some' professiographic records of teachers might not have the power to raise the motivation level of TE students to enter or stay in the teaching career. We believe that one of the most influential phenomenon that should be very closely interconnected with this picture of teachers' work load is the social status of teachers. In effectively functioning educational systems – such as Finland – the high demand on professionalism in the teaching profession goes hand in hand high social status.

The social status of teachers, seen from the point of view of financial reward in Slovakia in the last decades, has been much lower than in the cases of the other professions mentioned above. Maybe that was one of the reasons why there has been a long ongoing discussion among educational experts regarding the necessity of precisely and explicitly formulating the professional competencies and professional standards of the teaching profession. In 2007, the Slovak government approved *The Proposal of Professional Standards* as a starting document for the *Act on Pedagogical Employees* (Kasáčová et al, 2006). On the other hand, Finland does not have any precisely formulated professional standards of the teaching profession. In spite of that, the Finnish educational system is not the only system that belongs to one of the world's leaders in the academic performance of its students (e.g. in PISA tests). Teaching is Finland's 'most respected' profession, primary school teaching is even the most sought-after career. Teachers, including those teaching at primary level, are given the same status as doctors and lawyers. Primary school teaching belongs to the most popular professions among Finnish young people, "attracting the top quartile of high school graduates into highly selective university-based teacher training programmes" (OECD report on Finland, 2013).

There is yet another view of how to look at the social status of the teaching profession – and the TE students should be prompted to consider it. It is the social status seen from the angle of demands on this profession. According to recent international comparative research by Poliaková (2014, pp. 139–141), the profession of a primary school teacher is considered to belong to one of the most demanding professions (usually right on the second position after the profession of a doctor and before the profession of a lawyer). In this context (not paying attention to attractiveness and financial rewards as signs of social status), Poliaková's research confirmed previous research results showing that the idea of lowering the social status of the teaching profession had been a myth (Havlík & Koťa, 2007). Teachers themselves consider their profession to be demanding, and thus they themselves do not view it as of low social importance; rather, they view it as having quite high levels of social importance.

CONCLUSION

In the context of post-communist countries, a rapidly growing quantity – and in many cases also a growing quality – of research studies can be seen as an evidence of these countries' successful transition into a democratic system. In our book, we focused specifically on research on teachers, so called pedeutological research (*Part 1*).

One might expect to see an increase in the extent of pedeutological research during the last 25 years and, indeed, there has been such an increase. The first reason for this is, naturally, the longer time span available for researchers. Second, this increase might be seen as a consequence of the radical societal changes in 1989 from a massively state-controlled system of research to an open system that allows researchers to pursue their research questions and gain access to resources in a new, democratic way. (Of course, we are not mentioning here various organizational or economic limitations that researchers have to deal with.) So it should not surprise anybody that this publication had enough evidence to demonstrate that this expectation has been realized.

In comparison with the previous communist era, the period after 1989 has witnessed a boom of research, which has become so diverse that it was not in our 'power' – and it has not been our aim either – to produce a comprehensive list of all research studies. Rather we have focused here on presenting the main categories of research topics and methods, and then, to some extent, on providing brief comparisons. The main reason why we included all this information in *Part 2* and *Part 3* was to show the variability and the extent of pedeutological and, especially, of professiographic research on teachers. Afterwards, we sought overlaps with research in other developed countries. In *Part 4,* the intent was to provide details related to three special phenomena (teacher recruitment, feminization among teachers, and professional activities of teachers) in research on teachers.

To sum up the content of the current European trends of research on teachers, in general it can be said that it is currently focused on the professionalization of the teaching profession, and on teacher's professional competencies, knowledge and skills. It shows signs of both a withdrawal from academic orientation of education and a retreat from a simple practical training of teaching skills. Researchers have increasingly focused their attention on teachers as experts – their knowledge, their professional competencies, and their reflection. Investigators began to explore teachers' beliefs about teaching, their implicit and intuitive inclinations, images and emotions; their knowledge, thinking skills and ability to present logical, theoretical arguments; and, mainly, on their various relationships. "The research studies proved the decisive role of systematic theoretical reflection on practice in the design of teacher's personal and professional concept of one's own teaching" (Kosová, 2012, p. 38) which should be reflected in a balanced theoretical and practical preparation of TE students.

Our chosen strategy throughout the publication should be seen as a first attempt to produce a general picture of pedeutological research in a post-communist region, using mainly national data. We realize that within the limits of a single publication one cannot follow all the possible avenues of analysis of data from international resources (e.g. OECD TALIS reports, Visegrad Fund reports, various international statistics, etc.). The more limited purpose of this book was to sketch the contours and trends of research on teachers, using information from a limited number of countries. Thus, much work remains; there is room and a need for more questions and further investigations and comparisons with research on teachers in other regions and world cultures.

BIBLIOGRAPHY

Antalíková, Š, Kmec, J. 2012. *Prijímacie konanie na vysoké školy na ak. rok 2011/2012 v číslach a grafoch.* Bratislava : ÚIPŠ. [online] [ref. 2012-12-05]. Internet resource: http://www.uips.sk/sub/uips. sk/images/PKvs/Statista/r2011pk1.pdf.

Aparicio, C. C. & Arévalo, A. B. 2014. Teacher Training in Spain. In Pusztai, G., Engler, A. *Teacher Education Studies in Comparative Perspective.* Debrecen : CHERD, 2014, pp. 22–46.

Auerswald, F. 1956. *Pedagogická tvořivost a pedagogické čtení.* Prague : SPN.

Babiaková, S. 2008. *Kontinuálne profesijné vzdelávanie učiteľov.* Banská Bystrica : PF UMB.

Babiaková, S. & Tabačáková, P. 2009. Teoretické východiská profesiografie a tvorba výskumného nástroja. In Kasáčová, B., Cabanová, M. (eds.) *Učiteľ v preprimárnej a primárnej edukácii. Teória, výskumu, vývoj.* Banský Bystrica : PF UMB, pp. 179 - 202.

Babiaková, S., Cabanová, M. 2011. An Analysis of Teachers' Professional Activities in Slovakia. In Kasáčová, B., Babiaková, S., Cabanová, M. *Pre-Primary and Primary Teachers in Theory and Job-Analysis.* Banská Bystrica : PF UMB, pp. 103 – 128.

Babiaková, S., Cabanová, M., Doušková, A. 2011. Comparing the Findings of the Research into the Professional Activities of Slovak, Czech and Polish Teachers. In Kasáčová, B., Babiaková, S., Cabanová, M. *Pre-Primary and Primary Teachers in Theory and Job-Analysis.* Banská Bystrica : PF UMB, pp. 129 – 150.

Babiaková, S. 2012. Komparácia profesijných činností slovenských, českých a poľských učiteľov na primárnom stupni školy. *Pedagogická orientace,* Vol. 22, No. 2, pp. 222 - 242.

Baláž, O. 1972. K Výsledkom sociálne-pedagogického výskumu profilu mladého učiteľa. *Pedagogika,* Vol. 22, No. 2, pp. 147 – 165.

Baláž, O. 1973. *Učiteľ a spoločnosť.* Bratislava: SPN.

Baláž, O. 1975. Požiadavky vedeckotechnického pokroku a profil socialistického učiteľa. In *Socialistická škola a učiteľ v období vedeckotechnického rozvoja.* Bratislava : SPN, pp. 84 – 96.

Ball, S. J. 1981. *Beachside Comprehensive: A Case-Study of Secondary Schooling.* London : Routledge.

Bártková, H. 1981. Mikroanalýza vyučovacího procesu – aplikace metody A.A. Belacka. In *Interakce učitel – žáci, učitel – studenti.* Hradec Králové : PedF, pp. 130–135.

Bartošová, I., Faberová, M., Skutil, M. 2007. Koncepce pedagogické praxe primárního vzdělávání v přípravě učitelů. In *História, súčasnosť a perspektívy pedagogickej praxe v príprave učiteľov elementaristov.* Prešov: PdF PU.

Becker, H. S. 1953. The Teacher in the Authority System of the Public School. *Journal of Educational sociology: social climate as a factor in education,* Vol. 27, No. 3, pp. 128–141.

Benčo, J. 2001. *Metodológia vedeckého výskumu.* Bratislava: IRIS.

Bendl, S. 1997. Dotazníkové šetření o subjektivní obtížnosti učiteľských činností. *Pedagogika,* Vol. 47, No. 1, pp. 54-64.

Bendl, S. 2001. Percipování kázně ve škole učiteli a žáky. *Pedagogika,* Vol. 51, No. 2, pp. 206–216.

Beňo, M. et al. 1996. *Paradigma školy*. Bratislava : ÚIPŠ.

Beňo, M. et al. 2001. *Učiteľ v proces transformácie spoločnosti*. Bratislava: ÚIPŠ.

Beňo, M. et al. 2003. *Získavanie, rozvoj a udržiavanie efektívnosti učiteľov*. Bratislava : ÚIPŠ.

Beňová, M. 1972. Ideál učitele. In Fišer, J., Volný, J. *Osobnost učitele a učení*. Prague : UK.

Birzea, C. 1996. Reformní proces ve školství transformujících se zemí střední a východní Evropy. In *Reformy školství ve střední a východní Evropě*. Prague : UIV, pp. 7 – 14.

Blížkovský, B. 1959. Výchovný plán třídního učitele jako prostředek cílevědomé a soustavné výchovy. *Pedagogika*, Vol. 9, No. 2, pp. 212 - 236.

Blížkovský, B. 1967. Komplexní pojetí výchovně vzdělávací soustavy; její racionalizace, demokratizace, humanizace i řízení. In Blížkovský, B. *Výchovná soustava*. Prague. (Draft).

Blížkovský, B. 1980. *Projekt pedagogických profesí, specializací a kvalifikací pro československou výchovně vzdělávací soustavu*. Bratislava : SPN.

Blížkovský, B. 1990. On the Results and Trends in Pedeutological Research. In *Scientific and technological innovations and education for the world of tomorrow. Proceedings from the 10th Congress of W. A. E. VOL. in 1989*. Prague : WAER, pp. 404 – 410.

Blížkovský, B. & Kučerová, S. & Kurelová, M. et al. 2000. *Středoevropský učitel na prahu učící sa společnosti 21. Století. Vzdělávací situace, profesní činnosti a podmínky učitelů České, Slovenské a Polské republiky*. Brno : Konvoj.

Boledovič, S. 2013. *Slovenské školstvo očami rodičov, študentov, voličov, učiteľov.* Štúdia v rámci projektu „Aby každé dieťa na Slovensku malo výborného učiteľa a malo tak šancu rozvinúť svoj potenciál a v živote uspieť. "Manageria, October 2012. [online] [ref. 2012-12-06]. Internet: http://www.slideshare.net/Margo/slovensk-kolstvo-oami-rodiov-tudentov-voliov-uiteov

Borevskaya, N. 2007. The Russian Council of Comparative Education. In V. Masemann, M. Bray & M. Manzon (eds.), *Common Interests, Uncommon Goals: Histories of the World Council of Comparative Education Societies and its Members* (pp.299-308). Dordrecht & Hong Kong: Springer & Comparative Education Research Centre, The University of Hong Kong.

Bronfenbrenner, V. 1979. *The Ecology of Human Development : Experiments by nature and design.* Cambridge, MA : Harvard University Press.

Bureš, Z. 1981. *Psychologie práce a její užití.* Prague : Práce.

Burkovičová, R. 2006. *Přípravné vzdělávání učitelů mateřských škol.* Ostrava: PF OU.

Burkovičová, R. 2009. Profese učitele mateřské školy v proměnách času na území Čech a Moravy. In Kasáčová, B., Cabanová, M. (eds.) *Učiteľ v preprimárnej a primárnej edukácii : Teória, výskum, vývoj.* Banská Bystrica : PF UMB, pp. 117 – 140.

Burkovičová, R., Göbelová, T., Seberová, A. 2011. Analýza profesijných činností učiteľov v Česku. In Kasáčová, B., Babiaková, S., Cabanová, M. Filipiak, E., Seberová, A. et al. *Učiteľ preprimárneho a primárneho vzdelávania. : Profesiografia v slovensko-česko-poľskom výskume.* Banská Bystrica : PF UMB, pp. 231 – 284.

Byčkovský, P. 1983. *Základy měření výsledků výuky.* Prague : VÚIS, ČVUT.

Cach, J. 1968. Vývojové tendencie a problémy učitelského vzdělávání v poslednom padesátiletí. *Pedagogika,* Vol. 18, No. 6, pp. 777 – 805.

Cohen, L., Manion, M. & Morrison, K. 2007. *Research Methods in Education.* (6th edition). New York : Routledge.

Commission Staff Working Document. Supporting the Teaching Professions for Better Learning Outcomes. Communication from the Commission Rethinking Education: Investing in skills for better socio-economic outcomes. Strasbourg, 20.11.2012. 374 pp. [online] [ref. 2011-11-15]. Internet source: http://ec.europa.eu/education/news/rethinking/sw374_en.pdf

Creating Effective Teaching and Learning Environments: First Results from TALIS Executive summary. OECD, 2009. 32 pp. [online] [ref. 2010-11-15]. Internet source: http://www.oecd.org/edu/school/43044074.pdf, www.oecd.org/edu/TALIS.

Craig, Ch. J. 2009. Teacher Research and Teacher as Researcher. Vol. In Saha, L. J., Dworkin, A. G. (eds.) 2009. *International Handbook of Research on Teachers and Teaching. Springer IHRTT, vol 21.* New York : Springer Science+Business Media, 2009, pp. 61-70. [online] [ref. 2010-11-15]. Internet: http://www.springeVol.com/education/teachers+&+teaching/book/978-0-387-73316-6>.

Čára, V. et al. 1986. *Specifické problémy výchovně vzdělávacího procesu na základní škole a verifikace nového pojetí jejího obsahu.* Prague : SPN.

Černotová, M. 2000. Problémové prvky pregraduálnej prípravy učiteľov. In *Vzdelávanie pedagogických pracovníkov v 21. Storočí.* Bratislava : Metodické centrum, pp. 51-60.

Černotová, M. 2001. Študent učiteľstva – "peripetie" prípravy na fakulte". In Beňo, M. et al. *Učiteľ v procese transformácie spoločnosti.* Bratislava : UIPŠ.

Černotová, M., Drga, Ľ., Kasáčová, B., Lučák, J., Mäsiar, P., Pavlov, I., Valica, M. 2006. Koncepcia profesijného rozvoja učiteľov v kariérnom systéme. *Pedagogické rozhľady,* Vol. 15, No. 3, pp. 1–26.

Čižmáriková, K. 2015. Hodnoty budúcich učiteľov etickej výchovy. In Hanesová, D. *Research – Education – Evaluation.* Banská Bystrica : PF UMB, pp. 65 – 72.

Čížková, J. et al. 1988, *Struktura a integrace psychické zátěže u studentů učitelství.* In Učitelé a zdraví. Brno : Psychologické ústav AV ČR, pp. 75 – 83

Čulík, F. 1973. K některým podmínkám sociálně osobních postojů žáků k učiteli. In *Sborník prací pedagogické fakulty Univerzity Palackého v Olomouci.* Prague : SPN.

Cviková, J., Filadelfiová, J. 2008. Education through the Prism of Genders. Aspects of Key Risk. In *Gender Issues 2008* : Gender Sensitive Education in the Czech Republic, Poland, Slovak Republic and Ukraine. Warszawa : Heinrich Böll Stiftung, pp. 79 - 127.

Cviková, J., Filadelfiová, J. 2008. *Rodový pohľad na školstvo : Aspekty kľúčových rizík.* Dunajská Streda : Aspekt.

Daniel, J. Záťaž a jej zvládanie v profesii učiteľa. In *Pedagogická revue,* 2002, Vol. 54, No. 1, pp. 33 – 46.

Darák, M., Krajčová, N. 1995. *Empirický výskum v pedagogike.* Prešov: Manacom

Darák, M., Ferencová, J., Šuťáková, V. 2006. Pedagogická intervencia do rozvoja učebných kompetencií žiakov. In *Didaktika v dimenziách vedy a praxe.* Prešov : FHPV PU, UPP, PMC, pp. 113 – 117.

Dargová, J. 2001. *Tvorivé kompetencie učiteľa.* Prešov : Privatpress.

Disman, H. 1993. *Jak se vyrábí sociologická znalost.* Prague : Karolinum.

Doušková, A., Wágnerová, O. 2002. Pedagogická prax v systéme štúdia učiteľstva pre 1. stupeň ZŠ na PF UMB. In Kasáčová, B. (Ed.) *Spolupráca univerity a škôl. Zborník z konferencie Cvičný učiteľ.* Banská Bystrica : PF UMB, pp. 37-44.

Doušková, A., Porubský, Š. (eds.). 2004. *Vedenie študentov na odbornej praxi.* Banská Bystrica : PF UMB.

Doušková, A., Ľuptáková, K. (eds.) 2007. *Učiteľské kompetencie a pedagogická prax.* Banská Bystrica : PF UMB.

Doušková, A. 2008. *Na ceste k učiteľskej profesii.* Banská Bystrica : PF UMB.

Ďurič, L. 1969. *Výkonnosť a únava učiteľov vo vyučovacom procese.* Bratislava : SPN.

Dzierzgowska, A., Rutkowska, E. 2008. Blind to Gender: Equality Education the Polish Way. Report on Equality, Education in Primary, Grammar and Secondary Schools. In *Gender Issues 2008* : Gender Sensitive Education in the Czech Republic, Poland, Slovak Republic and Ukraine. Warszawa : Heinrich Böll Stiftung, pp. 47 - 76.

Education at a Glance 2012 : Highlights. OECD Publishing. 2012. [online] [ref. 2010-10-15]. Internet source: http://dx.doi.org/10.1787/eag_highlights-2012-en

Education at Glance 2013. OECD Indicators. Indicator D 5: Who are the teacher? [online] [ref. 2010-10-13]. Internet source: http://www.keepeek.com/Digital-Asset-Management/oecd/education/education-at-a-glance-2013/indicator-d5-who-are-the-teachers_eag-2013-29-en#page1

Education at a Glance 2014 : OECD Indicators. OECD Publishing. 566 pp. [online] [ref. 2010-11-15]. Internet source: http://www.oecd.org/edu/Education-at-a-Glance-2014.pdf

Eger, L., Čermák, J. 2000. Hodnocení burnout efektu u souboru českých učitelu. *Pedagogika,* Vol. 50, No. 1, pp. 65-69.

Engler, A., Kovács, E., Chanasová, Z. et al. 2014. Future Professional Plans of Students in Teacher Education. In Pusztai, G., Engler, Á. *Comparative Research on Teacher Education.* Ružomberok : Verbum, pp. 139 - 158.

Eurydice: *Key Data on Teachers and School Leaders,* forthcoming, provisional data. According to: http://ec.europa.eu/education/news/rethinking/sw374_en.pdf, pp. 10.

Fazis, U., Schmidt, B., Matas, M. 1994. *Arbeitszeitbelastungen Basler Oberlehrerinnen und Oberlehre.* Basel : Freiwillige Schulsynode.

Ferjenčík, J. 2000. *Úvod do metodologie psychologického výzkumu.* Prague : Portál.

Ferko, P. 1986. *Pohľad na prácu učitela fyziky.* Bratislava : SPN.

Fialová, I., Schneiderová, A. 1998. Syndrom vyhoření v profesní skupině středoškolských učitelu. In Řehulka, E., Řehulková O. (eds.) *Učitelé a zdraví.* Brno : Nakl. P. Křepela, pp. 55-66.

Filadelfiová, J. 2008. *Učiteľské povolanie : Aspekty rodovej rovnosti v škole.* Dunajská Streda : Aspekt. http://archiv.aspekt.sk/download/Rodovy%20pohlad%20na%20skolstvo.pdf

Filipiak, E., Lemańska-Lewandowska, Szymczak, J. 2011. Analýza profesijných činností učiteľov v Poľsku. In Kasáčová, B., Babiaková, S., Cabanová, M. Filipiak, E., Seberová, A. et al. *Učiteľ preprimárneho a primárneho vzdelávania : Profesiografia v slovensko-česko-poľskom výskume.* Banská Bystrica : PF UMB, pp. 285 – 314.

Fišer, J. 1966/67. Některé pokusy o typologii učitelovy osobnosti. *Socialistická škola,* Vol. 7, No. 3, pp. 157 – 164. & No. 4, pp. 221 – 228.

Flešková, M. 1997. Niektoré stresové situácie v práci učiteľa ZŠ. In Zborník Medacta. Nitra, No. 4, pp. 832 - 837.

Fónai, D. & Moldová Chovancová 2014. In Pusztai, G., Engler, Á., (eds.) *Comparative Research on Teacher Education.* Ružomberok : Verbum.

Forneck, H. J., Schriever, F. 2001. *Die individualisierte Profession: Einsichten aus einer Studie über Lehrerarbeitszeiten.* Giessen : Justus-Liebig-Universität.

Fülöpová, E. 1999. Profesijné činnosti učiteľa na Slovensku. In. *Slovenská pedagogika,* Vol. 2, 1999, No. 3-4, pp. 13-23

Furman, A. 1988. Návrh pozorovania činnosti učiteľa a žiaka na vyučovacích hodinách. *Psychológia a patopsychológia dieťaťa,* 23, No. 4, pp. 337 – 354.

Gage, N. L. (Vol. Ed.) 1963. *Handbook of Research on Teaching.* Chicago : Rand McNally

Gagné, R. M. 1975. *Podmínky učení.* Prague : SPN.

Galla, K. & Sedlář, R. et al. 1983. *Základy socialistické pedagogiky.* Prague : SPN.

Gallen, V., Karlenzig, B., Tamney, I. 1995. Teacher workload and work life in Saskatchewan. In *Education Quarterly Review,* (Statistics Canada, Catalogue no. 81-003-XPB), Vol.2, No.4, pp. 49-58.

Galton, M., MacBeath, J. et al. 2002. *A Life in Teaching? The Impact of Change on Primary Teachers' Working Life. A Report Commissioned by the National Union of Teachers Concerning Workloads in Primary Schools.* Cambridge : CU, Faculty of Education, 2002.

Gavora, P. 1986. *Výskumné metódy v pedagogika.* Bratislava : UK.

Gavora, P. 1987. Pravidlá komunikácie učiteľ – žiaci na základnej škole. *Pedagogika*, Vol. 37, No. 2, pp. 177-189.

Gavora, P. et al. 1988. *Pedagogická komunikácia v základnej škole.* Bratislava : Veda.

Gavora, P. 1994. Učiteľove viacnásobné otázky. *Pedagogika*, Vol. 44, No. 2, pp. 113–118.

Gavora, P. 1996. *Výskumné metódy v pedagogice.* Brno : Paido.

Gavora, P. 2001. Výskum životného príbehu: učiteľka Adamová. *Pedagogika*, Vol. 51, No. 3, pp. 352 – 368.

Gavora, P. 2002. Rozhodnutie stať sa učiteľom – pohľad kvalitatívneho výskumu. *Pedagogická revue,* Vol. 54, No. 3, pp. 240 – 256.

Gavora, P. 2004. Empirický výskum v časopise *Pedagogická revue* 1993 – 2003: Metodologické hľadisko. *Pedagogická revue,* Vol. 56, No. 2, pp. 145 – 161.

Gavora, P. 2007. *Sprievodca metodológiou kvalitatívneho výskumu.* Bratislava : UK.

Gavora, P. 2007. Vedci a učitelia – vzťah dvoch diskurzných komuník. In *Pedgogická revue,* 2007, Vol. 59, No. 2, pp. 115 – 130.

Gavora, P. et al. 2010. *Elektronická učebnica pedagogického výskumu.* Bratislava : UK. [online] [ref. 2016-04-05]. Internet resource: http:// www.e-metodologia.fedu.uniba.sk

Gavora, P. 2012. Rozvoj vnímanej zdatnosti (self-efficacy) študentov učiteľstva: možnosti zlepšenia učiteľského vzdelávania. *Aula*, Vol. 22, No. 2, pp. 62–77.

Gender Issues 2008 : Gender Sensitive Education in the Czech Republic, Poland, Slovak Republic and Ukraine. Warszawa : Heinrich Böll Stiftung.

Gender Sensitisation in the Educational Process at Elementary and Secondary Schools as Preparation for Future Job Desegregation (Programme of the European EQUAL Community Initiative) in cooperation with the Institute for Public Affairs and the FOCUS agency, Aspekt.

Gőbelová, T. 2006. *Axiologická dimenze ve výchově a vzdělávání.* Ostrava : Ostravská univerzita.

Gőbelová, T. 2009. Profese učitele primárního vzdělávání v České republice. In Kasáčová, B., Cabanová, M. (eds.) *Učitel v preprimárnej a primárnej edukácii. Teória, výskum, vývoj.* Banská Bystrica : PF UMB, pp. 64 – 65.

Gončarov, N. K. 1966. Metodologie a metódy výzkumu v pedagogice. *Pedagogika*, Vol. 16, No. 2, pp. 137-149.

Goodson, I. F., Hargreaves, A. 1996. *Teachers' Professional Lives.* London : Falmer Press.

Grumet, M. 1995. At home and in the classroom: The false comfort of false distinctions. In M. Ginsberg (Ed.) *The politics of educators' work and lives.* New York : Garland Publishing, Inc., pp. 55-72. In http://files.eric.Ed.gov/fulltext/ED432972.pdf.

Grumet, M., McCoy, K. 2000. Feminism and Education. In Moon, B., Brown, PP., Ben-Peretz, M. (eds.). *Routledge Internation Companion to Education*. London : Routledge, pp. 426 – 440.

Györgyi Z. et al. 2015. Nem formális tanulápp. In *Kozma Tamás és munkatársai: Tanuló régiók Magyarországon. Az elmélettől a valóságig*. Center for Higher Education Research and Development, pp. 107-143.

Halász, G. 2007. From Deconstruction to Systemic Reform: Educational Transformation in Hungary. *Orbis Scholae*, Vol. 1, No. 2, pp. 45 – 79.

Hanesová, D. 2009a. Výskumy o učiteľoch a profesionalizácii učiteľského povolania: bibliografia. (Research on Teachers and Professionalization of the Teaching Profession: Bibliography. In Kasáčová, B., Cabanová, M. *Učiteľ v preprimárnej a primárnej edukácii : teória, výskum, vývoj*. Banská Bystrica: Univerzita Mateja Bela, pp. 219-250.

Hanesová, D. 2009b. Komparatívny pohľad na výskum učiteľa a jeho profesijných činností. In Kasáčová, B., Cabanová, M. (eds.) *Profesia učiteľa v preprimárnej a primárnej edukácii v teórii a praxi*. Banská Bystrica : PF UMB, pp. 157 – 164.

Hanesová, D. 2011. Bibliographic Search. In Kasáčová, B., Babiaková, S., Cabanová, M. *Pre-Primary and Primary Teachers in Theory and Job-Analysis*. Banská Bystrica : PF UMB, pp. 155 - 168.

Hanesová, D. 2014. Teacher recruitment in Slovakia. In Pusztai, G., Engler, Á., (eds.) *Teacher Education Case Studies in Comparative Perspective*. Debrecen : Center for Higher Education Research and Development, pp. 107 – 130.

Hanesová, D. 2014b. Development of Research on Teachers and Their Professional Activities Before and after the Fall of Iron Curtain.

In *International journal of science, commerce and humanities*. South Shields : Tyne & Wear, Vol. 2, No. 4, pp. 166-191

Hanesová, D. 2015a. Predominance of Female Teachers in Central European Schools. In Pusztai, G., Engler, Á. & Markóczi, I. R. (eds.). *Development of Teacher Calling in Higher Education*. Budapest : Partium Press, pp. 160-178.

Hanesová, D. 2015b. What Should TE Students Know about the Reality of the Teaching Profession? In Pusztai, G., Ceglédi, T. (Eds.). *Professional Calling in Higher Education : Challenges of Teacher Education in the Carpathian Basin*. Budapest : Partium Press.

Hargašová, M. 1993. Ako sa adaptujú na vysokú školu slovenskí a americkí vysokoškoláci? In *Pedagogická revue*, Vol. 43, No. 7 – 8, pp. 421 – 435.

Hargreaves, A. 1986. *Two Cultures of Schooling: the case of middle schools*. Lewes : Falmer Pess, 1986.

Hargreaves, E. A. 2000. Four Ages of Professionalism and Professional Learning. In *Teachers and Teaching, History and Practice*, Vol. 6, No. 2, pp. 151 - 182.

Hargreaves, L., Cunningham, M. et al. 2007. *The Status of Teachers and the Teaching Profession in England: Views from Inside and Outside the Profession*. Final Report of the Teacher Status Project. Research report No. 831A. Cambridge : University of Cambridge. [online] [ref. 2010-04-25]. Internet resource: <http://www.educ.cam.ac.uk/research/pastprojects/teacherstatus/>

Harvey, A. S., Spinney, J. E. L. 2000. *Life On & Off the Job: Time-Use Study of Nova Scotia Teachers*. Nova Scotia : Saint-Mary's University.

Havel, J., Vlčková, K. 2004. Faktory a kontext rozvíjení profesních dovedností učitelů. In Havel, J., Janík, T. (eds.). *Pedagogická praxe v pregraduální příprave učitelů.* Brno: PedF MU, pp. 155–175.

Havlík, R. 1995. Motivace k učitelskému povolání. *Pedagogika*, 1995, Vol. 45, No.2, pp. 154–163.

Havlík, R. Spilková V. 1997. *Uplatnění absolventů vysokých škol – PedF UK.* Prague : PedF UK.

Havlík, R. 1998. Zrození učitele. In *Učitelské povolání z pohledu sociálních věd.* Prague : Pedagogická fakulta UK, pp. 78 - 90.

Havlík, R. 1998. Zrání učitele. In *Učitelské povolání z pohledu sociálních věd.* Prague : Pedagogická fakulta UK, pp. 91 - 110.

Havlík, R. 1999. Profesní „kariéra" a další vzdělávání v názorech a postojích učitelů. *Pedagogika*, Vol. 49, No. 2, pp. 147-155.

Havlík, R. 2000. Výskumy učitele a učitelské přípravy. In *Rozvoj národní vzdělanosti o vzdělávaní učitelu v evropském kontextu.* Prague : PdFUK.

Havlík, R., Koťa, J. 2007. *Sociologie výchovy a školy.* Prague : Portál.

Havlínová, M. 1993. Jak vypadá dnešní škola: jako dříve, nebo se mění? *Pedagogika*, Vol. 43, No. 2, pp. 137–148.

Hendl, J. 1999. *Úvod do kvalitativního výzkumu.* Prague: Karolinum.

Heřmanová, V., Langová, M. 2005. Inventář pro učitele a reflexe profesní činnosti učitelů. In Prokop, J., Rybičková, M. (eds.) *Proměny pedagogiky.* Prague: PdF UK, pp. 286-290.

Holik, I. 2008. The Role of Comparative Education in Hungary. In C. Wolhuter, N. Popov, M. Manzon & B. Leutwyler (Eds.),

Comparative Education at Universities World Wide (pp.81-87). Sofia: Bureau for Educational Services.

Horák, F. 1996. K aktuálním problémům začínajících učitelů. *Pedagogika,* Vol. 46, No. 4, pp. 245–255

Horká, H. 1999. Hodnotová kompetence jako jádro pedagogických kompetencí učitelů 1. stupne ZŠ. In *Premeny pedagogickej zložky učiteľa 1. stupňa ZŠ.* Banská Bystrica : PF UMB, pp. 45-54.

Horká, H. 2008. Hodnotová dimenze učitelského vzdělávání. In *Učitel a žák v současné škole.* první. Brno: Masarykova univerzita, 2008. pp. 94-104,

Hrabal, V. 1956. K otázce produktivnosti vyučovací hodiny. *Pedagogika,* Vol. 6, No. 4, pp. 445–451.

Hrabal, V., Lukš, J. 1971. Podíl osobnosti učitele na vytváření vztahu středoškoláků k vyučovacím předmětům. *Pedagogika,* Vol. 21, No. 2, pp. 261.

Hrabal, V. 1988. *Jaký jsem učitel?* Prague : SPN.

Hrdina, Ľ. 1987. K problematike dialógu v pedagogickej komunikácii. (The Problem of Dialogue in the Pedagogical Communication.) *Pedagogický výzkum,* No. 1, pp. 20 – 36.

Hrdina, Ľ. 1990. Dialogue and the Process of Teaching. In *Scientific and technological innovations and education for the world of tomorrow. Proceedings from the 10th Congress of W. A. E. VOL. in 1989.* Prague : WAER, pp. 350 – 354

Hrdina, Ľ. 1992. Dialóg a jeho účinnosť vo vyučovacom procese. *Pedagogika,* Vol. 42, No. 1, pp. 103-112.

Hroncová, J. 2001. Učiteľská profesia na Slovensku v kontexte transformačných zmien. In *Pedagogická profesia v kontexte aktuálnych spoločenských zmien.* Prešov : FHPV PU.

Hrubišková, H., Višváder, P. 2011. Sociokultúrne zázemie budúcich učiteľov prírodovedných predmetov. *Technológia vzdelávania, Vol. 19, No. 10, pp. 3–9.*

Hřebíček, L. 1995. Profesní vývoj adeptu učitelství. *Pedagogická orientace,* No. 17-18, pp. 70–77.

Hupková, D. 1987. *Empirická mikroanalýza spätnoväzbovej informácie vo výučbovej komunikácii na ZŠ a SŠ.* M.A. thesis. Bratislava : FF UK.

Hupková, M. 2006. *Profesijná sebareflexia učiteľov.* Nitra : PF UKF.

Janiš ml., K. 2014. Jak tedy reflektovat socialistickou pedagogiku? *Pedagogická orientace,* Vol. 24. No. 1, pp. 128–132.

Janik, T. 2005. *Znalost jako klíčová kategorie učitelského vzdelávání.* Brno : Paido.

Janík, T. 2007. Pedagogické znalosti jako součást profesní výbavy učitele. *Pedagogická orientace,* Vol. 4, No. 1, pp. 35-42.

Janík, T. 2009 *Možnosti rozvíjení didaktických znalostí obsahu u budoucích učitelů.* Brno : Paido, pp. 69-79.

Januška, Ľ. 1979. Profesiografický obraz učiteľa. *Jednotná škola,* Vol. 26, No. 2, pp. 117.

Jarešová, A. 2009. Historické podnety pre súčasné poňatie učiteľa predškolského vzdelávania na Slovensku. In Kasáčová, B., Cabanová, M. (eds.) *Učiteľ v preprimárnej a primárnej edukácii. Teória, výskum, vývoj.* Banská Bystrica : PF UMB, 2009, pp. 141 – 153.

Jersák, J. 1958. Kwartalnik pedagogiczny. *Pedagogika*, Vol. 8, No. 5, pp. 614-616.

Jesenková, D. 2008. *Rodová segregácia v príprave na povolanie.* APVV Project APVV-0726-07.

Juklová, K. 2008. Moje profesní já. In *Pedagogický výskum jako podpora proměny současní školy. Sborník.* Hrade Králové : Gaudeamupp.

Juklová, K. 2008. Moje profesní Já: profesní sebepojetí učitelů jako produkt sebereflexe jejich aktuálního vztahu k profesi. In *Pedagogický výzkum jako podpora proměny současné školy.* Sborník příspěvků z 16. konference ČAPV. Hradec Králové: Gaudeamus 2008. Jurovský, A., Jurovská, K. 1962. Individuálna výchovná práca v kolektívnej výchove. *Pedagogika*, Vol. 12, No. 1, pp. 23-42.

Jurovský, A., Jurovská, K. 1962. Individuálna výchovná práca v kolektívnej výchove. *Pedagogika*, Vol. 12, No. 1, pp. 23-42.

Juszczyk, S. 2003. *Metodológia empirických výskumov v spoločenských vedách.* Bratislava : IRIS.

Jyrhämä, H. 2013. *Finnish Teacher Education* (Lecture). Department of Teacher Education, University of Helsinki, Finland, 2013.

Kalous, J. et al. 1994. *Rozvoj vzdělávácí polotiky. Analytická evaluační studie.* Prague : program PHARE.

Kalhous, Z., Horák, F. 1996. K aktuálním problémům začínajících učitelů. *Pedagogika*, Vol. 46, No. 3, pp. 245 - 255.

Kane, R. 2008. *Perceptions of Teachers and Teaching: A Focus on Early Childhood.* [online] [ref. 2013-10-03]. Internet source: <http://www. educationcounts.govt.nz/publications/series/2535/26288/26247>

Kantorková, H. 1994. Potřeba změn v pedagogické přípravě učitelů primárního stupně školy. In *Učitel – jeho příprava a požadavky školské praxe.* Ústí nad Labem : Pdf UJEP, pp. 144–150.

Kantorková, H. 1998. Praktická pedagogická příprava studentů učitelství v alternatívním programu výuky pedagogiky. In *VI. Konference ČAPV.* České Budějovice : PdF JČU, pp. 141–147.

Kantorková, H. 2000. Studentské hodnocení inovovaného programu výuky pedagogiky. ... In *Pedagogický výskum v ČR.* Liberec : PdF TU, pp. 247-256.

Kariková, S. 1996. *Psychológia očami študentov PF.* Zborník príspevkov VIII. zjazdu slovenských psychológov. Bratislava: STIMUL.

Kariková, S. 1998, Humanizačné trendy vo vzdelávaní učiteľov. In *Zborník príspevkov „Nové trendy v pedagogicko-psychologickej príprave učiteľov".* Prešov : FHaPV, pp. 27 – 29.

Kariková, S. 1999. *Osobnosť učiteľa.* Banská Bystrica : PF UMB.

Kariková, S. 2000. Reakcia k úvodníku S. Štecha "Křivá huba nebo křivé zrcadlo?" Alebo Sú budúci učitelia stratenou generáciou? *Pedagogika,* Vol. 50, No. 3, pp. 285–287.

Kariková, S. 2002. Osobnostný profil študentov učiteľstva 1. st. ZŠ. In *Zborník vedecko -výskumných prác PF UMB, Acta universitatis Matthaei Belii.* Banská Bystrica : PF UMB.

Kariková, S. 2004. *Špecifiká profesijnej dráhy učiteliek.* Prešov : MPC v Prešove.

Kariková, S. 2005. *Vekové premeny učiteliek 1. stupňa základných škôl.* Banská Bystrica : PF UMB.

Kariková, S. 2005. Motivácia a fluktuácia v učiteľskej profesii. *Pedagogická revue,* Vol. 57, No. 3, pp. 284 - 293.

Kariková, S. 2010. Reflexia učiteľskej profesie v rozpätí 35 rokov. In *Acta Universitatis Matthaei Belii* No. 12. Banská Bystrica : PF UMB, pp. 57 – 70.

Kariková, S. 2015. Primary Education Teachers in the Biodromal Context. In Kasáčová, B., Kariková, S., Oelszlaeger-Kosturek, B. et al. *Teacher – Theoretical and Empirical Contexts of Primary Education.* Cieszyn : Wydawnictwo Galeria, pp. 11 – 32.

Kasáčová, B. 1996. Očakávania študentov od pedagogicko-psychologickej prípravy. *Pedagogická revue,* Vol. 48, No. 7 – 8, pp. 311- 317.

Kasáčová, B. 1998. Niekoľko poznámok k vzdelávaniu učiteľov 1. stupňa ZŠ. *Naša škola,* No.3, 1997/78, pp. 4– 7.

Kasáčová, B. 1999. Pedagogické spôsobilosti v kontexte prípravy učiteľov elementárnych škôl. In *Premeny pedagogickej zložky prípravy učiteľa 1. stupňa ZŠ.* Banská Bystrica : PF UMB, pp. 109-115.

Kasáčová, B. 2002. *Učiteľ – profesia a príprava.* Banská Bystrica : PF UMB.

Kasáčová, B. 2004. *Učiteľská profesia v trendoch teórie a praxe.* Prešov : MPC.

Kasáčová, B. 2005. *Reflexívna výučba a reflexia v príprave učiteľa.* Banská Bystrica : PF UMB.

Kasáčová, B., Kosová, B. 2006. Kompetencie a spôsobilosti učiteľa – európske trendy a slovenský prístup. In *Acta Universitatis Matthaei Belii: PF No. 10.* Banská Bystrica : PF UMB, 2006, pp. 15– 27.

Kasáčová, B., Kosová, B., Pavlov, I., Pupala, B., Valica, M. 2006. *Profesijný rozvoj učiteľa.* Prešov : MPC.

Kasáčová, B. 2009. Výskum učiteľskej profesie – reflexia, perspektívy a výzvy. In Kasáčová, B., Cabanová, M. (eds.) *Profesia učiteľa v preprimárnej a primárnej edukácii: v teórii a výskumoch.* Banská Bystrica : PF UMB, pp. 10–23.

Kasáčová, B. 2009. Zámer projektu APVV-0026-07: Profesia 'učiteľ predprimárnej edukácie' a 'učiteľ primárnej edukácie' v dynamickom poňatí. In Kasáčová, B., Cabanová, M. (eds.) *Učiteľ v preprimárnej a primárnej edukácii. Teória, výskum, vývoj.* Banská Bystrica : PF UMB, pp. 21 - 39.

Kasáčová, B., Cabanová, M. (eds.) 2009. *Učiteľ v preprimárnej a primárnej edukácii. Teória, výskum, vývoj.* Banská Bystrica : PF UMB.

Kasáčová, B. 2010. Introduction – about the Project No. APVV-0026-07. In Kasáčová, B. et a. *Teachers in Theory, Practice and Research.* Banská Bystrica : PF UMB, pp. 5-15.

Kasáčová, B., Tabačáková, P. 2010. Komparatívne výskumy o učiteľoch – teoretické východiská, možnosti a výzvy pre úvahy o učiteľoch primárneho vzdelávania. In Doušková, A., Porubský, Š., Huľová, Z. (eds.) *Učitelia a primárna edukácia včera, dnes a zajtra.* Banská Bystrica : PF UMB, pp. 109 – 119.

Kasáčová, B. 2011. The Methodology of the Project, the Research Issue, Objectives, Strategy, Tools and Procedures. In Kasáčová, B., Babiaková, S., Cabanová M. et al. *Pre-primary and Primary Teachers in Theory and Job-Analysis.* Banská Bystrica : PF UMB, pp. 83 – 99.

Kasáčová, B., Babiaková, S., Cabanová, M. et al. 2011. *Pre-Primary and Primary Teachers in Theory and Job-analysis.* Banská Bystrica : PF UMB.

Kasáčová, B., Babiaková, S., Cabanová, M., Filipiak, E., Seberová, A. et al. 2011. *Učiteľ preprimárneho a primárneho vzdelávania. Profesiografia v slovensko-česko-poľskom výskume.* Banská Bystrica : PF UMB.

Kasáčová, B. 2011. Výskumný problém, ciele a stratégia. In Kasáčová, B., Babiaková, S., Cabanová, M. Filipiak, E., Seberová, A. et al. *Učiteľ preprimárneho a primárneho vzdelávania. : Profesiografia v slovensko-česko-poľskom výskume.* Banská Bystrica : PF UMB, pp. 137 – 154.

Kasáčová, B., Tabačáková, P. 2011. Professiographic Research on Teachers. In Kasáčová, B., Babiaková, S., Cabanová M. et al. *Preprimary and Primary Teachers in Theory and Job-Analysis.* Banská Bystrica : PF UMB, pp. 68-81.

Kaslová, M. 1994. Model přípravy učitelů 1. Stupně ZŠ ... In *Stát se učitelem.* Prague : PedF UK, pp. 223–263.

Kasíková, H. 1995. Naučit se učit být učitelem. *Pedagogika,* Vol. 45, No. 5, pp. 429-447.

Kasíková, H. 2002. Učitel a jeho vzdělávací dráha: Snahy a obavy. Interpretace empirických dat z výzkumu na základní škole. In *Výzkum školy a učitele.* Sborník příspěvků 10. konference ČAPV. Prague: PdF UK.

Kebza, V., Šolcová, I. 1998. Burn-out syndrom : Teoretická východiska, diagnostické a intervenční možnosti. In *Československá psychologie,* Vol 42, No. 5, pp. 429 - 447

Kika, M. 2000. Pracovná spokojnosť pedagógov. *Pedagogické rozhľady,* Vol. 9, No. 4, pp. 1–5.

Kisselyova, O., Musiyenko, N. 2008. Gender-Sensitive Education in Ukraine: Achievements, Gaps and Challenges. In *Gender Issues*

2008 : Gender Sensitive Education in the Czech Republic, Poland, Slovak Republic and Ukraine. Warszawa : Heinrich Böll Stiftung, pp. 129 - 162.

Klímová, M. 1975. *Volba učitelství na pedagogických fakultách ČSR.* Prague : UK.

Klímová, M. 1986. *Studenti pedagogické fakulty UK v pohledu dlouhodobého výzkumu.* Prague : UK.

Kodým, M., Fitl, F. 1987. Podmínky úspěšnosti práce učitelů. In Langová, M., Kodým, M. et al. *Psychologie činnosti a osobnosti učitele.* Prague : Academia.

Kolláriková, Z. 1993. Fázy utvárania učiteľskej profesie. *Pedagogická revue,* Vol. 45, No. 9-10, pp. 483-493.

Komárik, E. 2002. *Metódy vedeckého poznávania človeka pre začiatočníkov.* Bratislava: UK.

König, H. 1967. K metodologickým problémům pedagogické vědy. *Pedagogika,* Vol. 17, No., 3, pp. 301 – 311.

Korim, V. 2011. Globalizačné a transformačné aspekty profesie učiteľa primárneho vzdelávania v Slovenskej republike. In Doušková, A., Porubský Š. *Problémy a perspektívy primárnej edukácie.* Banská Bystrica : PF UMB.

Kosová, B. 1996. *Hodnotenie ako prostriedok humanizácie školstva.* PhD. thesis. Bratislava : FiF UK.

Kosová, B. 1997. Humanistic Teaching Strategies in Primary Schools in Central Slovakia. Empirical Comparison of Traditional and Non-traditional Instruction. In *Humanisation Education – Paedagogica 14.* Bratislava : UK, pp. 91–103.

Kosová, B. 2000. *Humanizačné premeny výchovy a vzdelávania na 1. stupni ZŠ.* Banská Bystrica : MC.

Kosová, B. 2003. *Primárny stupeň vzdelávania v medzinárodnom porovnaní.* Banská Bystrica : PdF UMB.

Kosová, B., Pupala, B. 2004. Status, identita a profesijná spôsobilosť učiteľov. *Pedagogické rozhľady,* Vol. 13, No. 5, pp. 9–11.

Kosová, B. 2005. Perspektívy učiteľského vzdelávania – východiská, paradigmy a spoločenské výzvy. In *História, súčasnosť a perspektívy učiteľského vzdelávania.* Banská Bystrica : PF UMB, pp. 24–30.

Kosová, B. 2006. Profesia a profesionalita učiteľa. *Pedagogická revue,* Vol. 58, No. 1., pp. 1 – 14.

Kosová, B. 2006. Kríza učiteľskej profesie v medzinárodnom kontexte. In *Kríza učiteľskej profesie – Hľadanie riešení.* Banská Bystrica : MPC, pp. 7 – 16.

Kosová, B. 2009. Profesionalizácia učiteľskej profesie. In Kasáčová, B., Cabanová, M. eds. *Učiteľ v preprimárnej a primárnej edukácii. Teória, výskum, vývoj.* Banská Bystrica : PF UMB, 2009, pp. 11.

Kosová, B. 2010. Transformácia primárnej edukácie a vzdelávania jej učiteľov na Slovensku v zjednocujúcom sa európskom priestore. In Doušková, A., Porubský, Š., Huľová, Z. (eds.) *Učitelia a primárna edukácia včera, dnes a zajtra.* Banská Bystrica : PF UMB, pp. 32 - 43.

Kosová, B. 2011. Recent Trends of the profession in education policy and within a legislative framework. In Kasáčová, B., Babiaková, S., Cabanová, M. et al. *Pre-Primary and Primary Teachers in Theory and Job-analysis.* Banská Bystrica : PF UMB.

Kosová, B., Porubský, Š. 2011. *Transformačné premeny slovenského školstva.* Banská Bystrica : PF UMB.

Kosová, B. 2012. *Transformácia vysokoškolského vzdelávania učiteľov v kontexte reformy regionálneho školstva.* (Záverečná správa Rozvojového projektu MŠVVŠ v SR). Banská Bystrica : PF UMB.

Kosová, B., Tomengová, B. et al. 2015. *Profesijná pracktická príprava budúcich učiteľov.* Banská Bystrica : Belianum.

Koťa, J. 1998. Profesionalizace učitelského povolání. In Havlík, R., Koťa, J. et al. *Učitelské povolání z pohledu sociálních věd.* Prague : PedF UK, pp. 6–42.

Kotásek, J., Růžička, R. 1996. Sociální a profesní profil budoucích učitelů prvného stupně základní školy. *Pedagogika,* Vol 46, No. 2, pp. 168–180.

Koťátková, S., Průcha, J. 2013. *Předškolní pedagogika.* Prague : Portál.

Kraus, B. 1991. Hodnocení žáka z pohledu učitelů, rodičů a spolužáků. *Pedagogická revue,* Vol. 43, No. 7, pp. 507 – 515.

Krejčí, V. 1991. *Obecné základy pedagogiky.* Ostrava : PF.

Křesáková, H. 2001. *Změny ve struktuře a postojích uchazečů a studentů UK – Pedagogická fakulta v průběhu posledních 30 let.* Závěrečná práce. Prague: PedF UK.

Krystoň, M. 1994. *Pedagogicko-profesijná orientácia študentov stredných škôl na učiteľskú profesiu. (PhD thesis).* Banská Bystrica : PF UMB.

Kučera, M. 1992. Orientace školní etnografie. *Pedagogika,* Vol. 42, No. 4, pp. 455–464.

Kučera, M. 1994. Několik ukázek školní etnografie. *Pedagogika,* Vol. 44, No. 1, pp. 37–39.

Kučerová, S. 1987. *Profesionální činnosti a vzdělávání vedoucích pedagogických pracovníků.* Bratislava : SPN.

Kulič, V. 1980. Některá kritéria efektivity učení a vyučování a metody jejího zjišťování. *Pedagogika*, Vol. 30, no. 6, pp. 677 – 698.

Kurelová, M. 1997. Analýza profesionálních činností učitelů. In *ČAPV Výchova a vzdělávání v českých zemích na prahu třetího tisícletí.* Plzeň : PdF ZČU, pp. 167-176.

Kurelová, M. 1998. *Učitelská profese v teorii a v praxi.* Ostrava : PdF OU.

Kurelová, M. 2004. *Od profesiografie učitelů ke standardu učitelské kvalifikace.* Ostrava: PF OU.

Kurfürst, J. 1962. Jak posuzují žáci své učitele. In *Sborník prací Pedagogického institutu v Brně. Pedagogika – psychologie III.* Prague : SPN.

Langová, M., Kodým, M. et al. 1987. *Psychologie činnosti a osobnosti učitele.* Prague : Academia.

Langová, M., Kodým, M. et al. 1986. *Dovednostní model učitelovy profese.* Prague : OBIS PF UK.

Langová, M. et al. 1992. *Učitel v pedagogických situacích.* Prague : UK.

Landert, CH. 2002. *Die Arbeitszeit der Lehrpersonen in der Deutschschweiz, Ergebnisse einer einjährigen Erhebung bei 2500 Lehrerinnen und Lehrern verschiedener Schulstufen und Kantone.* Zürich : Landert Farago partner, 1999 and 2006. 55 pp. *Lehrerinen und Lehrer Schweiz LCH. Der Berufsautrag der Lehrerinnen und Lehrerl. Ein Handweiser zum Berufsautrag, zur Arbeitszeit und zum Arbeitspatz für Lehrpersonen.* Zürich : LCH.

Landert, CH. 2006. *Die Arbeitszeit der Lehrpersonen in der Deutschschweiz, Ergebnisse einer einjährigen Erhebung bei 2500 Lehrerinnen und Lehrern verschiedener Schulstufen und Kantone.* (2nd edition). [ref. 2015-09-06]. Zürich : LCH. [cit. 2008-09-13]. Internet source: <www.lch.ch>

Lapitka, M. 1985. Metódy a techniky výskumu. *Základy metodológie pedagogického výskumu.* Bratislava : SPN, pp. 51–77.

Lašek, J. 1995. Prvé skúsenosti s meraním klímy v škole a v učiteľskom zbore. In *Pedagogická revue,* 1995, Vol. 47, No. 1–2, pp. 43–50.

Lather, P. 1987. The absent presence: Patriarchy, capitalism, and the nature of teacher work. In *Teacher Education Quarterly,* Vol. 14, No. 2, pp. 25 - 38.

Lazarová, B. 2006. *Cesty dalšího vzdělávání učitelů.* Brno : Paido.

Leclercq, J. M. 1996. Učitelé v podmínkách společenských změn. In *Reformy školství ve střední a východní Evropě.* Prague : ÚIV, pp. 87 – 100.

LeCompte, M. 2009. Trends in Research on Teaching : An Historical and Critical Overview. In Saha, L. J., Dworkin, A. G. (eds.) *International Handbook of Research on Teachers and Teaching. Springer IHRTT, vol 21.* New York : Springer Science+Business Media, 2009, pp. 25 – 60. [online] [ref. 2008-09-25]. Internet resource: http://www.springer.com/education/teachers+&+teaching/book/978-0-387-73316-6>.

Liška, F. 1969. K sociálně psychologické problematice učitelského sboru. *Pedagogika,* Vol 19, No. 3, pp. 425 – 440. 17.

Lliška, F. 1970. K výzkumu interpersonálních vztahů v učitelském sboru. *Pedagogika,* Vol 20, No. 1, pp. 103 – 109.

Loukotka, J. 1966. Humanistická tradice naší pedagogiky. *Pedagogika*, Vol. 16, No. 1., pp. 1 – 17.

Lukas, J. 2007. Vývoj učitele : Přehled relevantních teorií a výzkumů (1. část). *Pedagogika*, Vol. 57, No. 4, pp. 36-49.

Lukas, J. 2008. Vývoj učitele : Přehled relevantních teorií a výzkumů (2. část). *Pedagogika*, Vol. 58, No. 1, pp. 36-49.

Lukášová-Kantorková, H. 2003. *Učitelská profese v primárním vzdělávání a pedagogická příprava učitelů.* Ostrava : OU.

Lukášová, H. 2004. *Bibliografie za období 1974-2004.* Ostrava: Repronis.

Lukášová, H. 2006. Metamorfózy pojetí učitelské přípravy a jejich pedagogický výzkum. *Pedagogika*, Vol. 56, No. 1, pp. 5-18.

Lukášová, H. 2009. Výzkum profese učitelství pro primární vzdělávání v České republice. In Kasáčová, B., Cabanová, M. (eds.). *Profesia učiteľ v preprimárnej a primárnej edukácii v teórii a výskumoch.* Banská Bystrica : PF UMB, pp. 31-40.

Macek, Z. 1990. A Contribution to Experimental Pedagogics. In *Scientific and technological innovations and education for the world of tomorrow. Proceedings from the 10th Congress of W. A. E. R. in 1989.* Prague : WAER, pp. 802 – 805.

Machalová, M. 1994. Integrující prvky v pregraduální přípravě učitelů primární školy. In *Problémy vzdelávania učiteľov 1. Stupňa.* Banská Bystrica : PF UMB, pp. 239–243.

Man, F., Mareš, J., Stuchlíková, I. 2000. Paradoxní účinky učitelových motivačních postupů. *Pedagogika*, Vol. 50, No. 3, pp. 224-235.

Maňák, J. 1992. *Problém domácích úkolů na základní škole.* Brno: Masarykova univerzita Brno

Maňák, J. 1994. *Nárys didaktiky.* Brno : MU.

Maňák, J. 2004. Didaktika 1964–2004. *Pedagogická orientace,* Vol. 15, No. 4, pp. 7–15.

Maňák, J. 2005. Minulost a přítomnost pedagogiky: Didaktika 1964-2004. *Pedagogická orientace,* Vol. 15, No. 4, pp. 7–15.

Maňák, J. 2013. Pedagogika a pedagógové v období vlády komunizmu. *Pedagogická orientace,* Vol. 23, No. 3, pp. 386 - 391.

Manzon, M. 2011. *Comparative Education: The Construction of a Field.* Hong Kong : Springer, The University of Hong Kong.

Mareš, J. 1975. Interakce učitel – žáci ve zjednodušeném modelu hromadného vyučování. *Pedagogika,* Vol. 25, No. 5, pp. 617 - 628.

Mareš, J. 1976. Využití televizní techniky při přípravě učitelů. *Pedagogika,* Vol. 26, No. 4, pp. 443-453.

Mareš, J. 1981. *Interakce učitel-žák, učitel-studenti.* Hradec Králové PF a Oš Vč KNV-

Mareš, J., Skalská, H. & Kantorková, H. 1994. Učitelova subjektivní odpovďenost za školní úspěšnost žáku. *Pedagogika,* Vol. 44, No. 1, pp. 25-35.

Mareš, J. 1985. Pedagogovy otázky a žákovy odpovědi. (Questions of the Teacher and Answers of the Pupil). *Odborná výchova,* Vol. 35, No. 6, pp. 168 – 174.

Mareš, J. 1991. *Studentské posuzování jako jedna z metod hodnocení vysokoškolské výuky.* Prague : SPN

Mareš, J., Křivohlavý, J. 1995. *Komunikace ve škole.* Brno : MU.

Mareš, J et al. 1996. *Učitelovo pojetí výuky.* Brno : MU.

Mareš, J. 2000. Pedagogickopsychologické práce publikované v časopise Pedagogika v letech 1951 – 2000. *Pedagogika,* Vol. 38, No. 4., pp. 365 – 405.

Mareš, J. 2010. O vstupování na tenký lEd. *Pedagogika,* Vol. 60, No. 2, pp. 99-103.

Maršalova, L., Mikšik, O. 1990. *Metodológia a metódy psychologického výskumu.* Bratislava : Slovenske pedagogicke nakladateľstvo.

Mazáčová, N. 2013. (Ne)štruktúrovaný model přípravy učitelu očima studentu. *E-Pedagogium,* No. 3, pp. 7 - 23.

Mihály, F. 2014. *Joghallgatók - Honnan jönnek és hová tartanak?* Debrecen: Debreceni Egyetem.

Milan, M. 1975. Príspevok ku štúdiu racionalizácie vyučovacej hodiny. *Jednotná škola,* No. 1, pp. 62.

Mikulová, D. 2006. Druhá etapa reformy slovenského školstva alebo Skončil sa čas vizonárov a nastal čas prakticej realizácie. In *Transformácia vzdelávania smerom k potrebám európskeho trhu práce (Fórum pedagogiky 2006).* Bratislava : MPC, pp. 10 – 34.

Mintrop, H. 1999. Changing Core Beliefs and Practices Trough Systemic Reform: The Case of Germany After the Fall of Socialism. *Educational Evaluation and Policy Analysis,* Vol. 21, No. 3, pp. 271 – 296.

Mistry, M., Sood, K. 2013. Why are there still so few men within Early Years in primary schools: views from male trainee teachers and male leaders? *Education 3-13: International Journal of Primary, Elementary and Early Years Education,* DOI:10.1080/03004279.20 12.759607.

Millenium. Národný program výchovy a vzdelávania v SR na najbližších 15 rokov. (National Program of Education in the Slovak Republic for 10 – 15 years – Project Millennium. 2002. Bratislava : IRIS.

Mlčák, Z. 1998. *Prosociální chování v kontextu dispozičních aspektů osobnosti.* Ostrava: OU.

Nelešovská, A. 1995. K přípravě učitelů prvního stupně základných škol. *Alma Mater,* No. 5-6, pp. 294–299.

Nelešovská, A., Kadlčíková, J. 2010. *Pohled absolventů oboru učitelství pro 1.st. ZŠ a učitelství pro MŠ na evropské kompetence.* Olomouc : Altyn.

Němec, J. 2005. Učitelé přípravných tříd v kontextu kvalitativního výzkumu. In *Pedagogický výzkum: reflexe společenských potřeb a očekávání?* Sborník příspěvků z XIII.konference ČAPV. Olomouc: PdF UJE, pp. 202-205.

Neugebauer, M., Helbig, M., Landmann, A. 2010. *Working Paper : Can the Teacher's Gender Explain the 'Boy Crisis' in Educational Attainment?* Arbeitspapiere – Working Papers Vol. 133. Mannheimer Zentrum für Europäische Sozialforschung. [online] [ref. 2011-04-25]. Internet resource: http://www.mzes.uni-mannheim.de/publications/wp/wp-133.

Nezvalová, D. 1994. Reflexe v pregraduální přípravě učitele. *Pedagogika,* Vol. 44, No. 3, pp. 241–245.

Nezvalová, D. 2002. Některé trendy v pedagogické přípravě budoucích učitelů. *Pedagogika,* Vol. 52, No. 3, pp. 309-320.

Ničkovič, R. 1968. *Metodológia pedagogického výskumu.* Bratislava : SPN.

Novotný, P. 1997. Autoritářství jako jedna z determinant výkonu učitelské profese. *Pedagogika,* Vol. 47, No. 3, pp. 247-258.

Novotová, J. 2008. Kompetence učitelů primární školy. In *Pedagogický výzkum jako podpora současné školy.* Hradec Králové : Gaudeamus, pp. 268-282.

Nowak, J. 2010. Preprimary Teacher' s Competences for Effective Education. In Kasáčová B. et al. *Teachers in Theory, Practice and Research.* Banská Bystrica : PF UMB.

Obdržálek, Z. 1990. From the Research of the Educational System Management in Czechoslovakia. In *Scientific and technological innovations and education for the world of tomorrow. Proceedings from the 10ᵗʰ Congress of W. A. E. R. in 1989.* Prague : WAER, pp. 452-460.

Obdržálek, Z. 1991. Analýza pracovnej zaťaženosti učiteľa. *Pedagogická revue,* Vol. 43, No. 7, pp. 498-505.

Omelka, F. 1955. Práce třídního učitele. *Pedagogika,* Vol. 5, No. 2, pp. 338-356.

Ondrejkovič, P., Verešová, M. 2003. Učiteľ a spoločnosť. *Pedagogická revue,* Vol. 55, No. 3, pp. 203 – 215.

Opatřil, S. et al. 1985. *Pedagogika pro učitelství prvního stupně základní školy.* Prague : SPN.

Opravilová, E. 2002. *Předškolní a primární pedagogika.* Liberec : TU v Liberci.

Osuská, Ľ. & Pupala, B. 1996. To je jako zázrak prírody: fotosyntéza v žiakovom poňatí. *Pedagogika,* Vol. 46, No. 3, pp. 214-223.

Ozga, J. (Ed.) 1988. *Schoolwork: approaches to the labour process of teaching.* Milton Keynes : OUP.

Pařízek, V. 1988. *Učitel a jeho povolání.* Prague : SPN.

Pašková, L., Valihorová, M. 2008. Výkonová motivácia študentov učiteľstva a študentov iných zameraní. In *Psychológia práce a organizácie.* Košice : Spoločenskovedný ústav SAV, 2008, pp. 162-165.

Pašková, L., Valihorová, M. 2010. Životná spokojnosť slovenských učiteľov rôznych typov škôl. *Pedagogická revue,* Vol 62, No. 1-2. Bratislava : Štátny pedagogický ústav.

Paton, G. 2013. Teaching in primary schools ‚still seen as a woman‘s job‘. *The Telegraph. 5.02.2013.* [online] [ref. 2014-04-25]. Internet: *http://www.telegraph.co.uk/education/educationnews/9849976/Teaching-in-primary-schools-still-seen-as-a-womans-job.html*

Paulík, K. 1999. *Psychologické aspekty pracovní spokojenosti učitelů.* Ostrava : OU.

Pavlovič, G. 1975. Učiteľ socialistickej epochy. In *Socialistická škola a učiteľ v období vedeckotechnického rozvoja.* Bratislava : SPN, pp. 67 – 71.

Pelikán, J., Lukš, J. 1973. *Příspěvek k problému závislosti úrovně interakce mezi učitelem a žákem na typu pedagogického působení.* Prague : Výzkumný ústav odborného školství.

Pelikán, J. 1998. *Základy empirického výzkumu pedagogických jevů.* Prague : Karolinum.

Píšová, M. 1999. *Novice Teacher.* University of Pardubice, Series C, Supplement 1.

Plichtová, J. 2002. *Metódy sociálnej psychológie zblízka. Kvalitatívne a kvantitatívne skúmanie sociálnych reprezentácií.* Bratislava : Média.

Pollard, A. 1985. *The Social World of the Primary school.* London : Holt Reinhart and Winston.

Poliach, V., Kariková, S. 1995. Psychometrická metóda výberu uchádzačov o vysokoškolské štúdium. *Acta Universitatis Matthae Belii.* Pedagogická fakulta No.2. Banská Bystrica: PF UMB, pp. 83-94.

Poliach, V. 1999. Situačná atribúcia u učiteľov ZŠ – problém pozitivity. In Hroncová, J., Bartík, J. (eds.) *Príprava učiteľov pre 21. storočie.* Banská Bystrica : PF UMB, pp. 151-161.

Poliach, V., Kariková, S., Valihorová, M. 1998. Učitelia "alternatívnych a tradičných škôl" – Podobnosti a rozdiely. *Pedagogické rozhľady,* Vol. 7, No. 1, pp. 8 – 10.

Poliaková, A. 2014. *Profesia učiteľa primárneho vzdelávania v medzinárodnej komparácii.* (Primary Teacher Profession in International Comparison). (PhD Thesis). Banská Bystrica : PF UMB.

Popov, N. 2007. The Bulgarian Comparative Education Society (BCES). In V. Masemann, M. Bray & M. Manzon (eds.), *Common Interests, Uncommon Goals:Histories of the World Council of Comparative Education Societies and its Members,* Hong Kong: Comparative Education Research Centre, The University of Hong Kong, and Dordrecht: Springer, pp.268-277.

Porubská, G. 1994. Profesionálna orientácia a výber uchádzačov na štúdium učiteľstva pre 1. Stupeň ZŠ. In *Zborník príspevkov "Problémy vzdelávania učiteľov 1. Stupňa ZŠ.* Banská Bystrica : PF UMB.

Porubská, G. 1997. Niektoré skúsenosti z ďalšieho vzdelávania pedagogických pracovníkov. In *K problematike ďalšieho vzdelávania pedagogických pracovníkov*. Bratislava : MC.

Porubský, Š., Kosová, B., Doušková, A., Trnka, M., Poliach, V., Fridrichová, P., Sabo, R., Adamcová, E., Lynch, Z., Cachovanová, R., Simanová, L. 2014. *Škola a kurikulum – transformácia v slovenskom kontexte*. Banská Bystrica : Belianum.

Portík, M. 2002. Reflexie začínajúcich učiteľov na úrovni praktickej prípravy počas štúdia. In Kasáčová, B. (Ed.) *Spolupráca univerzity a škôl*. Banská Bystrica : PF UMB, pp. 183-192.

Posch, P. 2004. Educational Innovations and Implications for the Teaching Force: The Case of Austria. In *Research Papers in Education* [online], Vol.19, No. 1, pp. 87 – 104. [online] [ref. 2009-04-25]. Internet resource: <http://www.informaworld.com/smpp/section?content=a713707792&fulltext=713240928#b15

Prax učiteľov slovenských škôl na nižšom sekundárnom stupni z pohľadu medzinárodného výskumu OECD TALIS 2008. Národná správa.2010. Bratislava : NÚCEM, 2008.

Prokešová, L. 1998. Rodiče, škola a začínající učitelé. *Rodina a škola* 45, No. 1, pp. 12.

Prokešová, L. 2000. Učitel základní školy a jeho problémy při nástupu do praxe. In *Učitel a jeho univerzitní vzdělávání na přelomu tisícletí*. Prague : PedF UK, pp. 205–210.

Provazník, K. et al. 1985. *Hygiena školní práce*. Prague : Avicenum.

Průcha, J. 1980. *Didaktická prognostika*. Prague : VÚOŠ.

Průcha, J. 1985. Pedagogický výzkum a pedagogická praxe: Aspekt využitelnosti vědeckých informací. *Pedagogika,* Vol. 35, No. 1, pp. 77 – 90.

Průcha, J. 1985. *Výzkum a teorie školní učebnice.* Prague : SPN.

Průcha, J. 1989. *Reálná výuka z pohledu učitelů a žáků. (Research report).* Prague : Pedagogický ústav J. A. K. ČSAV.

Průcha, J. 1989. Některé podmínky realizace obsahu vzdělání ve výuce. *Pedagogika,* Vol. 39, No. 2, pp. 121–138.

Průcha, J. 1990. *Pedagogický výzkum v zahraničí.* Prague : ÚŠI.

Průcha, J. 1995. Výzkum učitelské profese. *Alfa revue,* Vol. 5, No. 2, pp. 5–14.

Průcha, J. 1997. *Moderní pedagogika.* Prague: Portál.

Průcha, J. 1998. České základní vzdělávání: Nálezy pedagogického výzkumu. *Pedagogika,* Vol. 48, No. 3, pp. 212–243.

Průcha, J. 2000. 50 let časopisu Pedagogika: Vývoj media české pedagogické vědy. *Pedagogika,* Vol 50, No. 4, pp. 340 – 364.

Průcha, J. 2002a. *Moderní pedagogika.* 3rd Ed. Prague : Portal, 2002,

Průcha, J. 2002b. *Učitel. Současné poznatky o profesi.* Prague : Portál.

Průcha, J. 2002c. Vzdelávaní učitelů : Nové koncepce a diskuse v zahraničí. *Pedagogická revue,* Vol. 54, No. 5, pp. 401 – 417.

Průcha, J. 2011. Vstoupit, či nevstoupit na tenký led analýzy socialistické pedagogiky? *Pedagogika,* Vol. 61, No. 2, pp. 187 – 190.

Pstružinová, J. 1992. Některé pedagogicko-psychologické aspekty učiteľových otázek. *Pedagogika,* Vol. 42, No. 2., pp. 223-228.

Pusztai, G., Engler, Á., (eds.) 2014a. *Teacher Education Case Studies in Comparative Perspective.* Debrecen : HERD.

Pusztai, G., Engler, Á., (eds.) 2014b. *Comparative Research on Teacher Education.* Ružomberok : Verbum.

Pusztai, G., Ceglédi, T. (eds.) 2015. *Professional Calling in Higher Education : Challenges of Teacher Education in the Carpathian Basin.* Debrecen : Partium Press.

Pusztai, G., Engler, Á. & Markóczi, I. R. (eds.). 2015. *Development of Teacher Calling in Higher Education.* Budapest : Partium Press

Pýchová, I. 1993. K přínosu etnografické metody v pedagogickém výzkumu. *Pedagogika,* Vol. 43, No. 4, pp. 405–413.

Rabušincová, M., Pol, 1996. M. Vzťahy školy a rodiny dnes: hledání cest k partnerství (2). *Pedagogika,* Vol. 46, No. 2, pp. 105 – 11.

Řehulka, E., Řehulková O. 1988. Problematika tělesné a psychické zátěže při výkonu učitelského povolání. In Řehulka, E., Řehulková, O. (eds.) *Učitelé a zdraví.* Brno : Nakl. P. Křepela, pp. 99-104.

Řehulka, E., Řehulková O. (eds.) 1998. Zvládání zátěžových situací a některé jejich důsledky u učitelek. In *Učitelé a zdraví.* Brno : Nakl. P. Křepela, pp. 106-111.

Rendl, M. 2004. Učitel v žákovském diskursu. *Pedagogika,* Vol. 44, No. 4, pp. 347-354.

Richardson, W. (Ed.) 2001. *Handbook of Research on Teaching.* 4. ed. Washington, D.C. : American Educational Research Association.

Ritomský, A. 2002. *Metódy psychologického výskumu: Kvantitatívna analýza dát.* Bratislava : MSŠR.

Rosa, V., Turek, I., Zelina, M. 2000. *Návrh koncepcie výchovy a vzdelávania v SR: Projekt Milénium.* Nitra : Slovdidac.

Rýdl, K. 2008. Kvalita vzdělávání učitelů v Evropě. Standardizace nové role učitele? In *Pedagogická evaluace 08 Sociália.* Ostrava : PdF OU, pp. 2-8.

Saha, L. J., Dworkin, A. G. (eds.) 2009. *International Handbook of Research on Teachers and Teaching. Springer IHRTT, Vol 21.* New York : Springer Science+Business Media, 2009. 1219 pp. [online] [ref. 2010-04-25]. Internet: Rhttp://www.springer.com/education/ teachers+&+teaching/book/978-0-387-73316-6>

Samuhelová, M., Tokárová, M. 1996. Profesionálna etika a jej špecifiká v pedagogickej činnosti učiteľa. *Pedagogické spektrum*, Vol. 5. No. 6, pp. 11-23.

Schnitzerová, E. 1994. Postoje študentov učiteľských fakúlt k budúcemu povolaniu. *Pedagogická revue,* Vol. 46, No. 7-8, pp. 337-349.

Schnitzerová, E. 1994. Vývoj postojov k učiteľskému povolaniu. *Psychológia.* Banská Bystrica : PF UMB, pp. 30-38.

Schnitzerová, E. 1995. Profesijné postoje budúcich učiteľov k svojmu povolaniu. *Pedagogické spektrum*, Vol. 2, No. 1, pp. 49-57.

Schreiner, P., Spinder, H., Vos, F. (eds.) 1995. *Education and Europe: Bildung und Europa.* Münster, Utrecht : ICCS, ECCE, EFTRE, IV.

Schreiner, P., Spinder, H., Taylor, J., Weterman, W. (eds.) 2002. *Committed to Europe's Future: Contribution from Education and Religious Education.* Münster : CoGREE, Comenius-Institut.

Schubert, J. 1987. Štyridsať rokov vzdelávania učiteľov na pedagogických fakultách v Československu. *Jednotná škola,* Vol. 39, No. 7, pp. 641-655.

Seberová, A. 2006. *Výskumná kompetence v učitelské profesi a ve vzdělávání učitelu.* Ostrava : PF OU.

Seberová, A. 2009. Učitelská profese v primárním vzdělávání pohledem pedagogického výzkumu v ČR. In Kasáčová, B., Cabanová, M. eds. *Učiteľ v preprimárnej a primárnej edukácii. Teória, výskum, vývoj.* Banská Bystrica : PF UMB, pp. 201 – 217.

Seberová, A. 2009. Pracovní spokojenost učitelů v teoretických reflexích a výsledcích pilotní fáze výzkumu. In Kasáčová, B., Cabanová, M. (eds.) *Profesia učiteľa v preprimárnej a primárnej edukácii: v teórii a výskumoch.* Banská Bystrica : PF UMB.

Semerádová, V. 1994. Povolání učitele z perspektivy žáka. *Pedagogika,* Vol. 44, No. 4, pp. 342-346.

Silova, I. 2009. The Crisis of the Post-Soviet Teaching Profession in the Caucasus and Central Asia. *Research in Comparative and International Education,* Vol. 4, No. 4, pp. 366 – 383.

Šimíčková-Čížková, J. et al. 2008. *Přehled vývojové psychologie.* Olomouc: Univerzita Palackého v Olomouci.

Šimičková, H. 2001. Názory učitelů na integrované vyučování v primární škole. In *Pedagogická orientace,* No. 4, pp. 40 – 53.

Šimoník, O. 1994, 1995. *Začínající učitel.* Brno : Masarykova univerzita.

Singer, S., Nielsen, N., Schweingruber, H. (eds.) 2012. *Discipline-Based Education Research: Understanding and Improving Learning.* Washington : National Academies Press.

Skalková-Procházková, J., Skalka, J. 1963. K metodologickým otázkám naší pedagogické vědy. *Pedagogika*, Vol. 13, No. 3, pp. 257 - 271.

Skalková, J. et al. 1993. *Úvod do metodologie a metod pedagogického výzkumu*. Prague : SPN.

Skalková, J. 1990. Perspectives of Changes in the Process of Education in the Czechoslovak school. In *Scientific and technological innovations and education for the world of tomorrow*. Proceedings from the 10th Congress of W. A. E. R. in 1989. Prague : WAER, pp. 162–166.

Slavík, J., Čapková, D. 1994. Reflexe učitelské profese: Divadlo, dílna a těžký život v pojetí výuky. *Pedagogika*, Vol. 44, No. 4, pp. 377–388.

Slavík, J., Siňor, S. 1993. Kompetence učitele v reflektování výuky. *Pedagogika*, Vol. 43, No. 2, pp. 155-164.

Solfronk, J. et al. 2000. *Učitelství jako profese*. Liberec : TU v Liberci.

Somr, M., & Hrušková, L. 2014. Herbart's philosophy of pedagogy and educational teaching. *Studia Edukacyjne*, *33*, 413–429.

Špendla, V. 1974. *Učiteľ a učiteľská profesia*. Bratislava : SPN.

Špendla, V. 1975. Pedagogická sociológia v učiteľskom vzdelávaní. In *Štúdie o učiteľskom vzdelávaní (Studies on Teacher Education)*, pp. 15–77.

Spilková, V., Uhlířová, J. 1991. Současný stav primární školy ve vybraných evrobpských zemích. *Alfa revue*, Vol. 1, No. 3, pp. 42-48.

Spilková, V., Uhlířová, J. 1992. Základní tendence učitelského vzdělávání v zemích EPP. *K pojetí přípravy učitelů školy prvního stupně*. Prague : Karolinum, pp. 131–135.

Spilková, V. 1994. Alternativní model přípravy učitelů 1. stupně zákldní školy. In *Stát se učitelem*. Prague : PdF UK.

Spilková, V. 1998. Transformace učitelské přípravy na PdF UK Prague – vize a skutečnost. In *ČAPV*. Ústí nad Labem : PdF UJEP, pp. 73–78.

Spilková, V. et al. 1996. *Didaktická východiská primárního vzdělávaání detí na základní škole*. Prague : PdF UK.

Spilková, V. 1997. *Proměny primární školy a vzdělávání učitelů v historicko-srovnávací perspektivě*. Prague : PF UK.

Spilková, V. et al. 2004. *Současné proměny vzdělávání učitelů*. Brno : Paido.

Spilková, V. 1996. Východiska vzdělávání učitelu primárních škol. *Pedagogika*, Vol. 46, No. 2, pp. 135-146.

Spilková, V. et al. 1999. *Univerzitní vzdělávání učitelů primární školy na prelomu století*. Prague : PdF UK.

Spilková, V. 2007. Učitelská profese v měnících se požadavcích na vzdělávání. *Pedagogika*, Vol. 57, No. 4, pp. 338–348.

Spilková, V., Vašutová, J. 2008. *Učitelská profese v měnících se požadavcích na vzdělávání*. Prague : UK.

Strausss, A., Corbin, J. 1999. *Základy kvalitativního výzkumu : postupy a techniky metody zakotvené teorie*. Boskovice : Albert.

Štech, S. 1994. Co je to učitelství a lze se mu naučit? *Pedagogika*, Vol. 44, No. 4, pp. 310–320.

Štech, S. 1998. Dilemata a ambivalence učitelského povolání. In Havlík, R. et al. *Učitelské povolání z pohledu sociálních věd*. Prague : PF UK, pp. 43-59.

Štech, S. 2000. Křivá huba, nebo křivé zrcadlo? *Pedagogika,* Vol. 50, No. 2, pp. 117–120.

Štefanovič, J. 1967. *Psychológia vzťahu medzi učiteľom a žiakom.* Bratislava : SPN.

Štefanovič, J. 1974. *Psychológia učiteľovho pedagogického taktu.* Bratislava : SPN.

Stránská, Z., Poledňová, I. 2005. Prediktory syndromu vyhoření u učitelů. In. *Pedagogický výzkum: reflexe společenských potřeb a očekávání?* Sborník příspěvků z XIII.konference ČAPV. Olomouc: PdF UJEP, 2005, pp. 283 - 286.

Střelec, S. 1996. Teorie a praxe rodinne vychovy ve studiu učitelstvi. In *Pedagogická orientace,* No. 18 – 19, pp. 120 – 122

Stuchlíková, I. 2006. Role implicitních procesů při utváření profesní identity budoucích učitelů. *Pedagogika,* Vol 56, No.1, pp. 31-44. *Štúdie o učiteľskom vzdelávaní (Studies on Teacher Education) 1975*

Šturma, J. 1986. K problematice popisu a třídění didaktických dovedností. In *Dovednostní model učitelovy profese.* Prague : PedF UK, pp. 86–130.

Šulc, O. 1987. *Prognostika od A po Z.* Prague : NTL.

Švaříček, R., Šeďová, K. (eds.). 2007. Kvalitativní výzkum v pedagogických vědách. Prague: Portál.

Švec, Š. 1988. *Didaktika I.* Bratislava : FiF UK.

Švec, Š. 1993. Koncepcia humanitisticky orientovanej výučby. *Pedagogická revue,* Vol. 45, No. 1-2, pp. 2–15.

Švec, Š. 1998. *Základné pojmy v pedagogike a andragogike.* Bratislava : IRIS.

Švec, Š. Et al. 2000. *Metodológia vied o výchove. Kvantitatívno-scientické a kvalitatívno-humanitné prístupy.* Bratislava : IRIS.

Švec, Š. 2002. *Základné pojmy v pedagogike a andragogike.* Bratislava : IRIS.

Švec, Š. et al. 2009. *Metodológia vied o výchove.* Bratislava : IRIS.

Švec, Š. 2010. Súčasný pedagogický výskum na Slovensku. In *Pedagogická orientace,* Vol. 20, No. 2, pp. 23-39.

Švec, V. 1995. Význam diagnostiky učitelova pojetí výuky v jeho pregraduální přípravě. *Pedagogika,* Vo. 45, No. 2, pp. 164–170.

Švec, V. 1996. Sebereflektivní deníky a studentské posuzování výuky. In *Pedagogická evaluace v podmínkách současné školy.* Olomouc : ČAPV, pp. 96–99.

Švec, V. 1999. *Monitorování a rozvoj pedagogických dovedností.* Brno : Paido.

Švec, V., & Musil, J. 1999. Pokus o změnu přístupu k osvojování pedagogických vědomostí a dovedností studentů učitelství (ve výuce obecné didaktiky). In T. Svatoš (Ed.), *Poslední desetiletí v českém a zahraničním pedagogickém výzkumu.* Hradec Králové: Česká asociace pedagogického výzkumu a Pedagogická fakulta VŠPP, pp. 268–274.

Švec, V. (Ed.) 2000. *Monitorování a rozvoj pedagogických dovedností.* Brno : Paido.

Švec, V. et al. 2002. *Cesty k učitelské profesi: utváření a rozvíjení pedagogických dovedností.* Brno : Paido.

Švec, V., Musil, J. Vliv pedagogických intervencí na změnu studentova pojetí výuky. *Pedagogická orientace*, 2003, No. 2, pp. 71–82.

Švec, V. 2005. *Pedagogické znalosti: teorie a praxe.* Prague : ASPI Publishing.

Svatoš, T., Mareš, J. (eds.). 1993. *Pedagogická interakce a komunikace.* Hradec Králové: Gaudeamus

Svatoš, T. 1995. Flandersova metoda interakční analýzy v učitelské přípravě. *Pedagogika,* Vol. 45, No. 1, pp. 64–70.

Svatoš, T. 1999. *Jak absolventi reflektují svou pregraduální učitelskou přípravu.* Hradec Králové : PdF VŠPP.

Svatoš, T. 2002. Studentské portfolio učitelském studiu. In Walterová, E. et al. *Výzkum školy a učitele.* Prague : PdF UK. CD.

Svatoš, T. 2010. Aby pedagogika byla vědou provázenou historickou sebereflexí. *Pedagogika,* Vol. 60, No. 1, pp. 1–3.

Taborsky, E. 1961. *Communism in Czechoslovakia, 1948–1960.* York : Princeton University Press.

Tichá, M. 1995. Sociálně ekonomické postavení studentů PedF UK. *Alma mater,* Vol. 5, No. 5-6., pp. 307 – 316.

Tichá, M. 1999. Sociálne ekonomické postavení a ekonomické aspirace studentů PedF UK. IN *Učitelské povolání z pohledu sociálních vEd.* Prague : PedF UK, pp. 111-121.

Tollingerová, D. 1972. *Formální jazyk jako prostředek hlubšího poznání vyučovacího procesu. Referát na medzin. konferencii INTERPROGRAMMA.* Smolenice.

Trachsler, E., Inversini, P. et al. 2003. M. *Arbeitsbedingungen, Belastungen und Ressourcen der Thurgauer Volksschullerkräfte.* Thurgau : Pädagogische Hochschule.

Travers, R. M. W. (Ed.) 1973. *Second Handbook of Research on Teaching.* Chicago : Rand McNally, AERA.

Troman, G. 1996. The Rise of the New Professionals: the restructuring of primary teachers' work and professionalism. In *British Journal of Sociology of Education*, Vol. 17, No. 4, pp. 473 – 487.

Troman, G. 2007. Annex : Research on teachers' work and teaching professionalism: a short history. In Hextall, I., Gewirtz, PP., Cribb, A., Mahony, P. *Changing Teacher Roles, Identities and Professionalism : An Annotated Bibliography.* London : TLRP (Teacher and Learning Research Programme, Roehampton University, King's College London), 2007, pp. 30 – 49.

Turek, I. 1996. *O niektorých súčasných koncepciách vyučovacieho procesu.* Banská Bystrica : MC.

Turek, I. 1998. *Zvyšovanie efektívnosti vyučovania.* Bratislava : Metodické centrum.

Turek, I. 1999. Postoje vysokoškolských učiteľov k ich pedagogicko-psychologickej príprave. In *Schola 99.* Bratislava : KIPP STU.

Uhlířová, J. 2011. Vzdělávání učitelů pro primármí školu (1. stupeň) po 2. světové válce v proměnách času (do Vol. 1989). *Pedagogika,* Vol. 61, No. 4, pp. 344 – 357.

Urbánek, P. 1999. Profesní časové zatížení učitelu ZŠ. *Pedagogika,* Vol 49, No. 3, pp. 277-288.

Urbánek, P. 2000. Sebehodnocení úrovně profesijních činností studentů učitelství. In V. Švec (Ed.) *Monitorování a rozvoj pedagogických dovedností.* Brno : Paido, pp. 137-147.

Urbánek, P. 2001. Podpora práce učitelů ve světle současných problémů učitelství. In *Učitelé jako profesní skupina, jejich vzdělávání a podpůrný system.* Prague : PdF UK.

Urbánek, P. 2005. *Vybrané problémy učitelské profese.* Liberec : PedF TU.

Václavík, J. 1972. *Veda, prax a škola.* Bratislava : SPN.

Václavík, V. 1995. *Cesta ke svobodné škole.* Hradec Králové : Gaudeamus.

Václavík, V. et al. 1997. *Otevřené vyučování – na příkladu vzdělávacícho programu pro 3. Vol. ZŠ.* Prague : Strom.

Valica, M. 2001. Pracovná spokojnosť učiteľov stredných škôl na Slovensku, v Čechách a niektorých krajinách. In *Pedagogické rozhľady*, Vol. 10, No. 4, pp. 6-8.

Valica, M. 2002. Výskum o učiteľovi pre učiteľa. *Pedagogické rozhľady*, Vol. 11, No. 4, pp. 1-3.

Valicová, T. 2006. Motivácia k voľbe štúdia u učiteľov 1. stupňa. *Pedagogické rozhľady*, Vol. 15, No. 2, pp. 33-34.

Valihorová, M., Glázerová, I. 1994. Výskum osobnostných a intelektových predpokladov pre učiteľské povolanie. In *Psychológia.* Banská Bystrica : PF UMB, pp. 14-29.

Valihorová, M. 1995. K psychologickým otázkam výberu učiteľov 1. stupňa ZŠ. In *Teorie v pedagogické praxi, praxe v pedagogické teorii v učitelském studiu.* Brno : Paido, pp. 89-91.

Valihorová, M. 2009. Spokojnosť a kvalita života budúcich učiteľov = Satisfaction and wellbeing of future teachers. In *Učiteľ pre školu 21. storočia*. Banská Bystrica : PF UMB, pp. 438-454.

Valkovičová, M. 2008. Adaptácia a profesionálny rozvoj začínajúceho učiteľa. *Pedagogické rozhľady*, Vol. 17, No. 5, pp. 5 – 16.

Váňa, J. 1960. Ke kritice naší pedagogické vědy. *Pedagogika*, Vol. 10, No.1, pp. 1-3.

Váňa, J. 1962. O metodologických problémech v rozvoji pedagogické teorie. *Pedagogika*, Vol. 12, No. 3, pp. 272-315.

Vaněk, J. 1947. *Průhledy učitelstvím*. Brno : Komenium.

Vaněk, J. 1967. *O nedostatečném vztahu naši pedagogické teorie k praxi*. Bratislava : ČSAV.

Vašina, M., Valošková, M. 1998. Učitel – pracovní zátěž – zdraví. In Řehulka, E., Řehulková, O. (eds.). *Učitelé a zdraví 1*. Brno : Nakl. P. Křepela, pp. 7–25.

Vašutová, J., Švecová, J. 1999. Profese učitele, její problémy a perspektívy. In VAŠUTOVÁ, J. et al. *Vybrané otázky vysokoškolské pedagogiky*. Prague : PF UK, pp. 48–77.

Vašutová, J. 2001. Kvalifikační předpoklady pro nové role učitelů. In *Učitelé jako profesní skupina, jejich vzdělávání a podpůrný systém*. Sborník 1.díl. Prague: PdF UK.

Vašutová, J. 2004. *Profese učitele v českém vzdělávácím kontextu*. Brno : Paido.

Vašutová, J. 2007. *Být učitelem. Co by měl učitel vědět o své profesi*. Prague: PdF UK.

Velikanič, J. 1967. *Výskumné metódy v pedagogike a pedagogicko-psychologická diagnostika.* Bratislava: SPN.

Velikanič, J. et al. 1978. *Pedagogika pre pedagogické fakulty vysokých škôl.* Bratislava : SPN.

Višňovský, Ľ. 2000. *Triedny učiteľ.* Banská Bystrica : PF UMB.

Višňovský, Ľ., Kačáni, V. 2002. *Základy školskej pedagogiky.* Bratislava : IRIS.

Višňovský, Ľ., Babicová, Z. 2012. *Triedny učiteľ a spolupráca školy s rodinou.* Banská Bystrica : PF UMB.

Vorlíček, Ch. 1984. *Úvod do teorie výchovy.* Prague : SPN.

Vorlíček, Ch. 1979. *Úvod do pedagogiky.* Prague : SPN.

Waller, R. 1969. *Sociology of Teaching.* In Lortie, D. C. The balance of control and autonomy in elementary school teaching. In *The Semi-Professions and Their Organization.* Toronto: The Free Press, pp. 1-53.

Walterová, E. (Ed.) 2001. *Učitelé jako profesní skupina, jejich vzdělávání a podpůrný systém.* Prague : PedF UK.

Walterová, E. 2002. Učitelé : Proměny profese a rekonstrukcie jejich vzdělávání. *Pedagogická revue,* Vol. 54, No. 3, pp. 220 – 239.

Walterová, E. 2007. The Comparative Education Section in the Czech Pedagogical Society. In Masemann, V., Bray, M. & Manzon, M. eds. *Common Interests, Uncommon Goals...* Dordrecht & Hong Kong: Springer, CERC, The University of Hong Kong, pp. 256 – 267.

Walterová, E. 2008. Comparative Education for Teachers in the Czech Republic: Aims, Models, Problems. In C. Wolhuter, N. Popov,

M. Manzon & B. Leutwyler (eds.), *Comparative Education at Universities World Wide*. Sofia: Bureau for Educational Services, pp. 42-46.

Waterkamp, D. 2007. Section for International and Intercultural Comparative Education. In V. Masemann, M. Bray & M. Manzon (eds.), *Common Interests, Uncommon Goals: Histories of the World Council of Comparative Education Societies and its Members* (pp.139-154). Dordrecht & Hong Kong: Springer & Comparative Education Research Centre, The University of Hong Kong, pp. 139-154

Webb, R. *Primary School Teachers' Work. Special Interest Group on Group on ASPE/BERA*. [. [online] [ref. 2010-04-25]. Internet resource:. <http://www.aspe-uk.eu/furtherinfo.asp>

Webb, R., Vulliamy, G., Hämäläinen, P., Sarja, A. et al. 2004. A Comparative Analysis of Primary Teaching professionalism in England and Finland. In *Comparative Education*, Vol. 40, pp. 83 – 107.

Webber, P., Liikanen, I. 2001. Introduction. In *Education and Civic Culture in Post-communist countries: Studies in Russia and Eastern Europe*. Basingstoke : Palgrave.

Wittrock, M. C. (Vol. Ed.)1986. *Handbook of Research on Teaching : A Project of the American Educational Research Association*. (3. Ed.) New York : MacMillan Publ. Comp.,. 1037 pp.

Woods, P. 1979. *The Divided School*. London: Routledge and Kegan Paul.

Zelina, M., Furman, A. 1986. Metodika psychologickej analýzy vyučovacích hodín. *Psychológia a patopsychológia dieťaťa*, Vol. 21, No. 4, pp. 321 – 332.

Zelina, M. 1994. Pokus o vymedzenie konceptu stratégie tvorivej edukácie. In Jurčová, M., Zelina, M. (eds.). *Kreativizácia a jej bariéry.* Bratislava : ÚEP, SAV, pp. 91-100.

Zelina, M. 1997. *Tvorivý učiteľ.* Bratislava : Metodické centrum.

Zelinová, M. 1998. Učiteľ a burnout efekt. *Pedagogika,* Vol. 48, No. 2, pp. 164-169.

Zimová, L. 1997. Uplatňování absolventů PF UJEP v praxi. *Pedagogika,* Vol. 47, No. 3, pp. 269–276.

Žiaková, E. 1996. Problémy vysokoškolských študentov 1. ročníka pri ich adaptácii na vysokoškolské štúdium. *Pedagogická revue,* Vol. 48, No. 7-8, pp. 354-363..

Žilínek, M. 1997. *Etos a utváranie mravnej identity osobnosti.* Bratislava : IRIS.

Internet websites:

http://www.nuv.cz/vse-o-nuv/vyzkumny-ustav-pedagogicky-vup-1

http://ec.europa.eu/education/news/rethinking/sw374_en.pdf, pp. 31

http://www.uippp.sk/prehlady-skol/statisticka-rocenka---zakladne-skoly

http://www.nucem.sk/documents//27/medzinarodne_merania/talis/publikacie/TALIS-web.pdf

http://archiv.aspekt.sk/download/Rodovy%20pohlad%20na%20skolstvo.pdf

http://archiv.aspekt.sk/download/Ucitelske_povolanie_summary.pdf

http://data.uipp.unesco.org/

http://ec.europa.eu/eurostat/statistics-explained/index.php/
Education_statistics#Entry_into_tertiary_education

http://www.esfem.sk/UserContent/File/jesenkova_rodova%20
segregacia.pdf

www.focus-research.sk

www.ivo.sk

http://www.msmt.cz/vzdelavani/skolstvi-v-cr/statistika-skolstvi/
genderova-problematika-zamestnancu-ve-skolstvi

http://www.ncee.org/programs-affiliates/center-on-international-
education-benchmarking/top-performing-countries/finland-
overview/finland-teacher-and-principal-quality/

www.oecd.org/edu/TALIS

http://www.oecd.org/pisa/pisaproducts/46581035.pdf,

http://www.oecd.org/edu/Finland_EAG2013%20Country%20
Note.pdf

http://www.esfem.sk/UserContent/File/jesenkova_rodova%20
segregacia.pdf

http://www.ruzovyamodrysvet.sk/chillout5_items/1/0/3/5/1035
_fd805f.pdf

http://www.telegraph.co.uk/education/educationnews/9849976/
Teaching-in-primary-schools-still-seen-as-a-womans-job.html

http://www.tradingeconomicpp.com

http://www.uippp.sk/prehlady-skol/statisticka-rocenka---zakladne-skoly

http://ec.europa.eu/education/news/rethinking/sw374_en.pdf, pp. 29.

http://www.keepeek.com/Digital-Asset-Management/oecd/education/education-at-a-glance-2013/indicator-d5-who-are-the-teachers_eag-2013-29-en#page1;   http://www.nucem.sk/documents//27/medzinarodne_merania/talis/publikacie/TALIS-web.pdf

http://www.keepeek.com/Digital-Asset-Management/oecd/education/education-at-a-glance-2013/indicator-d5-who-are-the-teachers_eag-2013-29-en#page1;   http://www.nucem.sk/documents//27/medzinarodne_merania/talis/publikacie/TALIS-web.pdf

http://www.tradingeconomicpp.com;   http://data.uipp.unesco.org/index.aspx?queryid=178

http://www.educationalrev.upp.edu.pl/

APPENDICES

APPENDICES

APPENDIX NO. 1

Daily professiographic record of a teacher

Source: Kasáčová, B. 2011. The Methodology of the Project, the Research Issue, Objectives, Strategy, Tools and Procedures. In Kasáčová, B., Babiaková, S., Cabanová M. et al. *Pre-primary and Primary Teachers in Theory and Job-Analysis*. Banská Bystrica: PF UMB, pp. 83–99.

Categories of activities	Time intervals									
A. Activities directly connected with teaching, lesson preparation	7,00-8,00	8,00-9,00	9,00-10,00	10,00-11,00	11,00-12,00	12,00-13,00	13,00-14,00	14,00-15,00	15,00-16,00	16,0 and later
designing and planning of lessons										
checking up pupils' preparedness for lessons										
motivating, activating students										
explaining new subject matter										
...										
B. Other activities connected with education	7,00-8,00	8,00-9,00	9,00-10,0	10,00-11,00	11,00-12,00	12,00-13,00	13,00-14,00	14,00-15,00	15,00-16,00	16-...
meetings with parents										
doing paper work										
staff meetings										
break supervision										
...										

	7,00-8,00	8,00-9,00	9,00 -10,0	10,00- 11,00	11,00- 12,00	12,00- 13,00	13,00- 14,00	14,00- 15,00	15,00- 16,00	16 - ...
C. Activities connected **with other roles of T**										
membership in commitees										
school librarian										
organizing school club										
...										
D. Education and self-education										
taking part in education										
self-study										
E. Extracurricular and public activities of T										
F. Others:										
....										

Appendix No. 2

Daily activities of pre-primary school teachers

Source: Babiaková, S., Cabanová, M. 2011. An Analysis of Teachers' Professional Activities in Slovakia. In Kasáčová, B., Babiaková, S., Cabanová, M. *Pre-Primary and Primary Teachers in Theory and Job-Analysis*. Banská Bystrica : PF UMB, pp. 103–128.

A. *Activities directly connected with teaching, lesson preparation*

a1 – projecting and planning the educational activities

a2 – preparation and organizing the learning environment

a3 – activities evoking activation, motivation

a4 – performing teaching, management of educational activities inside the school

a5 – setting up and solving various educational situations/conflicts etc.

a6 – performing and managing educational activities outside the school

a7 – performing and managing educational activities on the school playgrounds

a8 – assessment of the results of learning

a9 – individual care for children with special educational needs

a10 – creating teaching aids

B. *Other activities connected with educational processes*

a11 – diagnosing the children

a12 – meetings and cooperation with parents

a13 – doing paperwork

a14 – consultations with other teachers, school psychologists etc. about individual students a15 – staff meetings

a16 – assisting children with activities connected with self-service and keeping daily regime

a17 – supervision during children's autonomous activities, games and resting time

C. *Activities connected with other functions/roles of the teacher*

a18 – service on various committees (methodological, advisory, etc.)

a19 – school librarian/library management

a20 – leading a club for children

a21 – keeping school records, chronicles, archives etc.

a22 – keeping a school cabinet, taking care of a classroom premises

D. *Education and self-education*

a23 – participant in a course/further education

a24 – self-study

a25 – teaching other colleagues

E. *Off-school, public/community activities connected with teaching profession:* a) with children: organizing performance of children - organizing Children's Day, Mother's Day, teachers' choir, etc.; b) without children: attending community meetings/conferences, fundraising, school projects, preparing new school curriculum, administrative activities, or planting trees.

F. *Other activities:* a) without children: organizing exhibitions of children's art work, decorating the rooms, buying rewards for children, website management, preparing video/photo presentation of the school, fundraising, management of various events – swimming training course, preparation of parental ball, masquerade, writing school newspaper, etc.; b) with children: preparing various performances - trips, preparing children for competitions, visiting public library, etc.

APPENDIX No. 3

Daily activities of primary school teachers

Source: Babiaková, S. 2012. Komparácia profesijných činností slovenských, českých a poľských učiteľov na primárnom stupni školy. *Pedagogická orientace,* Vol. 22, No. 2, pp. 222–242.

A. *Activities directly connected with teaching, lesson preparation*

a1 – projecting and planning of the lesson

a2 – checking up pupils' preparedness for lessons

a3 – activities evoking activation, motivation

a4 – explaining new subject matter

a5 – managing and coordination of students' learning activities

a6 – testing of learning results

a7 – assessment – in direct contact with pupils

a8 – preparation/teaching individual plans for students with special educational needs

a9 – recognizing and solving behavioral situations

a10 – marking and grading students' assignments

a11 – creating teaching aids

B. *Other activities connected with education process*

a12 – diagnosing students

a13 – meetings and cooperation with parents

a14 – doing paperwork

a15 – consultations with other teachers, school psychologists etc. about individual students

a16 – staff meetings

a17 – supervision of students (in classrooms, school halls and other premises, canteen)

C. *Activities connected with other functions/roles of the teacher*

a18 – member of various committees (methodological, advisory, etc.)
a19 – school librarian
a20 – leading a club for students
a21 – keeping school chronicles, archives etc.
a22 – keeping a school cabinet

D. *Education and self-education*

a23 – participant of a course/further education
a24 – self-study
a25 – teaching other colleagues

E. *Off-school, public/community activities connected with teaching profession* (similar sort of activities as at ISCED 0)

F. *Other activities* (decorating school, collecting money or teaching aids, fundraising, restructuring school curricula, etc.)

APPENDIX NO. 4

Themes of pedeutological research in post-communist countries

Titles of studies included in *New Educational Review* (a Czech-Polish-Slovak journal):

Research focus	Researcher	Nationality	Year of publ.
Motivation and fluctuation in teacher's profession	Soňa Kariková	Slovak	2003
Analysis of 216 research studies from Proceedings of Czech Association of Pedagogical Research	Hana Lukášová-Kantorková	Czech	2003
Inquires into responsibilities of teacher	Joanna M. Michalak	Polish	2005
Teacher profession age particularities	S. Kariková	Slovak	2005
Creative and emotional competence of contemporary teachers	Beata Dyrda, Irena Przybylska	Polish	2005

Teachers' Constructions of Citizenship and Enterprise: Using Associative Group Analysis with Teachers in Hungary, Slovenia and England	Alistair Ross, Barbara Read, Marjanca Pergar Kuscer, Marta Fülöp, Cveta Pucko, Mihaly Berkics, Monika Sándor, Merryn Hutchings	Slovenian, Hungarian, English	2005
Values Preferred by Teachers and Students for Teacher Training Faculties	Janusz Stanek	Polish	2005
Research on Teacher Professional Development	Michaela Píšová	Czech	2005
Coping with Misbehaviour and Discipline – the Teachers' Perspective	Jacek Pyzalski	Polish	2005
Teaching Goals and an Analysis of Teaching Projects	Alena Doušková	Slovak	2006
Teachers' Professional Development and Burnout Syndrome	Sabina Koczoń-Zurek	Polish	2007
Life Perspectives of Teachers in Poland and the United States	Carol A. Radich, David Bolton	Polish, American	2007
Prospective Teachers' Attitudes to their Profession	Jan Lašek, Šárka Wiesenbergová	Czech	2007

- Preparation for the Further Education of Music Education Teachers in Active Practice	Belo Felix, Marianna Kološtová	Slovak	2007
Teachers' perception of their competences and professional education - empirical study	Beata Dyrda, Irena Przybylska	Polish	2007
Research into Career Stories of Teachers of the 1st Level of Primary Schools	Simoneta Babiaková	Slovak	2008
Foreign Language Teacher Education: Th e Polish Case	Hanife Akar	Turkish	2009
Following the Path of the Teacher's Development Joint reflection	Alena Hošpesová, Marie Tichá	Czech	2009
Quality of Life among Primary School Teachers and other Professions	Jitka Šimíčková-Čížková, Bohumil Vašina	Czech	2009
The Problem of Theory and Practice in University Course Theory and Methods of Literacy Development	Branislav Pupala, Zuzana Petrová	Slovak	2009
Future Teachers' Knowledge and Awareness of their Role in Student Misbehaviour	Mateja Pšunder	Slovenian	2009

Life Satisfaction of Slovak Teachers Depending on the School Type	Lucia Pašková, Marta Valihorová -	Slovak	2010
School Culture - Teacher`s Competence - Students` Creative Attitudes. Reflection on school pragmatics	Barbara Dobrowolska	Polish	2010
Teaching[1]Learning? A longitudinal Study into the Efl Teacher Trainees` Cognitions	Grażyna Kiliańska-Przybyło	Polish	2010
The Teacher`s Conception of Project-based Teaching	Jana Kratochvílová	Czech	2010
Slovak Pre-Service Teacher Self-Efficacy: Theoretical and Research Considerations	Peter Gavora	Slovak	2010
The Teacher`s Conception of Project-based Teaching	Jana Kratochvílová	Czech	2010
The Teacher`s Entering the Professional Career - What Can Teachers` Autobiographies Reveal (to us)	Marija Javornik Krečič	Slovenian	2010
Reflections on the Teaching Profession Over the Last Thirty-Five Years	Soňa Kariková	Slovak	2010

Preconditions for Effective Teaching (in the Light of Data from the TALIS 2008 Project - Polish Perspective)	Rafał Piwowarski	Polish	2010
Teachers' Personal Qualities as the Determinants of Their Empathetic Abilities	Beata Pituła, Małgorzata Kitlińska-Król	Polish	2010
Maths Lessons - Are They Gender Neutral in the Polish Perspective? Report on the Third Stage of Research	Dorota Turska, Ryszarda Ewa Bernacka	Polish	2010
Investigation of Prospective Teachers' Approaches to Learning in Biology and Ecology	Michaela Píšová, Klára Kostková	Czech	2011
Crucial Determinants Affecting the Attitude of Czech Educators toward Education of Extraordinarily Gift ed Learners	Šárka Portešová, Marie Budíková, Helena Koutková	Czech	2011
Pupil, Pros and Cons of Teacher's Motivation	Jitka Šimíčková-Čížková	Czech	2011
Significant Aspects of Professional Orientation of Beginning Teachers	Kateřina Juklová	Czech	2011
Teaching for Multicultural Sensitivity: Who Does It Best?	Eva Konečnik Kotnik, Marija Javornik Krečič	Slovenian	2011
Teachers' Role Perception	Irena Przybylska	Polish	2011

Research on Professional Values of Primary Student Teachers - Results of Mixed Model Research	Taťána Göbelová	Czech	2011
Application of the Scientific Method in the Integrated Science Teaching	Stanko Cvjeticanin, Mirjana Segedinac, Vlasta Sucevic	Serbian	2011
Teaching Styles in Teachers Educating Romany Pupils	Erika Novotná, Milan Portik	Slovak	2012
Teachers` Preparation for Work in the Environment of Multiculturalism - a Research Report	Alina Szczurek-Boruta	Polish	2012
The Attitudes of Pupils to Teachers According to the Gender Differences	Nikola Sklenářová	Czech	2012
The Attitudes of Academic Teachers as Well as Education Students Towards the Categories of Values Relativised in the Postmodern Culture	Magdalena Kleszcz, Małgorzata Łączyk	Polish	2012
From the Research on Teachers` Professional Identity	Beata Pituła	Polish	2012
Job Satisfaction and Stress among Teachers	Karel Paulík	Czech	2012

Professional Activities of Primary Education Teachers in International Comparison	Simoneta Babiaková	Slovak	2012
Effects of Teacher Trainers Interventions during Students` Pre-School Teaching Practice	Alena Doušková, Marian Trnka	Slovak	2012
Observing Teachers` Emotional Expression in Their Interaction with Students	Simona Prosen, Helena Smrtnik Vitulić, Olga Poljšak Škraban	Slovenian	2013
Occupational Mental Stress Assessment of Elementary School Teachers and Firefighters – Rescuers	Olga Šušoliaková, Jindra Šmejkalová, Markéta Papršteinová Milan Reboš	Czech	2013
Educational Strategies of Teachers with Various Senses of Efficacy	Mariola Chomczyńska-Rubacha, Krzysztof Rubacha	Polish	2013
Types of Consciousness of English Teachers in Lower Secondary Schools in the Light of Paulo Freire`s Theory	Milena Gucma	Polish	2013
Teachers` Information Competence and Use of ICT Methods and Tools - Research Report	Eunika Baron-Polańczyk	Polish	2013

Ethical Orientations and Sex in Teachers with Varied Educational Strategies	Krzysztof Rubacha, Mariola Chomczyńska-Rubacha -	Polish	2013
Influence of Profession on Teachers' Quality of Life	Olga Šušoliaková, Jindra Šmejkalová, Markéta Papršteinová, Lenka Hodačová, Eva Čermáková	Czech	2013
Social Experiences of Future Teachers - a Research Report	Alina Szczurek-Boruta	Polish	2013
Researching the Association between Teachers and School Outcomes (Based on TALIS Data and Lower Secondary School Examination Results)	Rafał Piwowarski	Polish	2013
Pre-service Mathematics Teachers' Financial Literacy	Vladimíra Petrášková	Slovak	2013
Subjective Evaluation of Demands on Performance of Teacher Professional Activities	Lenka Rovňanová		2013
Primary School Teachers' Professional Performance in the Czech Republic, Bulgaria and Poland.	Beata Pituła, Wiesława A. Sacher	Polish, Bulgarian	2014

Analysis of the Implementation of Practical Work in the Area of Early Science Education of Primary School Pupils in the Republic of Slovenia	Irena Delčnjak Smrečnik, Samo Fošnarič, Branka Čagran -	Slovenian	2014
Influence of Head Teacher's Leadership Style on Tutor Satisfaction	Nebojsa Pavlovic	Serbian	2014
Expert Teachers' Interactive Cognition: an Analysis of Stimulated Recall Interviews	František Tůma, Michaela Píšová, Petr Najvar, Věra Janíková	Czech	2014
Perceived Autonomy Levels among Elementary School Students and Their Teachers	Maja Matrić, Katja Košir	Slovenian	2014
Myths about Gift ed Learners from the Perspective of Teachers	Šárka Portešová, Marie Budíková, Dana Juhová	Czech	2014
Teacher as an Authority? Supporting the Student's Sense of Belonging to the School Community as a Condition for Their Development and the Teacher's Success in Educating	Beata Pituła, Agnieszka Wilczyńska	Polish	2014
Verbal and Visual Strategies of Teachers' Work on Identity	Roman Švaříček	Czech	2014

Pedagogical Condition at Undergraduate Teacher Preparation	Andrysová Pavla, Martincová Jana, Hana Včelařová	Czech	2014
Emotional Intelligence as a Predisposition to Pursue the Teaching Profession	Anna Romanowska-Tołłoczko, Bianka Lewandowska	Polish	2014
Communicative Competence Development for Future Teachers	Tatyana Noskova, Tatiana Pavlova, Olga Yakovleva, Nina Sharova	Russian	2014
Influences of a Short Term International Field Experience on Preservice Teachers` Perceptions and Cultural Competency	Betsy Kanarowski, Susan S. Johnston	USA, Polish	2014
Multidimensionality of Learning - a Report from some Studies Among Candidates for Teachers	Alina Szczurek-Boruta	Polish	2014
The Principal's Behaviors and Job Satisfaction Among Middle School Teachers	Aleksandra Tłuœciak-Deliowska, Urszula Dernowska -	Polish	2015
The 'Nervousness' Factor in the Personality Profile of Teachers in the Slovak Republic	Soňa Kariková, Terézia Rohn	Slovak	2015
Mentor Teacher Training in the Light of a Study at the University of Szeged	Alice Dombi, Krisztina Kovács	Hungarian	2015

Process Orientation of the Conception of Student Learning	Marija Javornik Krečič, Eva Konečnik Kotnik, Jernej Kovač	Slovenian	2015
Everyday Professional Life Experiences of Teachers in the Midlife Transition Period	Jiří Prokop, Joanna M. Łukasik	Czech, Polish	2015
Labeling in the Education of Gifted Pupils	Eva Machů, Ilona Kočvarová, Tereza Císlerová	Czech	2015
Self-Assessment of the Social Competence of Teacher Education Students	Snježana Dubovicki, Maja Brust Nemet	Croatian	2015
„How and Why Should I Study?": Metacognitive Learning Strategies and Motivational Beliefs as Important Predictors of Academic Performance of Student Teachers	Sonja Čotar Konrad	Slovenian	2015

APPENDIX NO. 5

Synchronic view - Examples of professiographic research

Source: Hanesová, D. 2009. Výskumy o učiteľoch a profesionalizácii učiteľského povolania: bibliografia. In Kasáčová, B., Cabanová, M. *Učiteľ v preprimárnej a primárnej edukácii : teória, výskum, vývoj.* Banská Bystrica: Univerzita Mateja Bela, pp. 219–250.

Countries	Institutions	Projects/research on teaching profession	Added information
Austria	Bundesministerium für Unterricht und Kunst, Bundesministerium für Bildung, Bundes-ministerium für Finanzen, Bundesministerium für öffentliche Leistung und Sport, Institut für Unter-nehmensberatung und die Kooperations partner Institute for Social Research and Analysis (SORA), Klinische Abteilung Arbeitsmedizin am Allgemeinen Krankenhaus, Wien Klagenfurt Universität	Research of workload, contentment and health of primary and secondary school teachers Arbeitszeit, Zufriedenheit, Beanspruchungen und Gesundheit der LehrerInnen in Österreich in 2 phases: April – July; August – September) – diaries of teachers in 2-weeks long periods (notes about the beginning and the duration of each activity chosen out of a pre-prepared catalogue of activities). Teaching profession, workload of teachers.	1999–2000: Doblhamer, M. et al 2004: Posch, P.
Australia	Australian Education Union; Australian Association for Research in Education (AARE); Edith Cowan University, Department of Education	The characteristics of the profession of early childhood teachers, professiograms, redefining teaching profession and teacher competence (ISCED 1 teacher of all subjects). In 2001 - project Teacher Competency Framework (Level 1): questionnaires, focus groups. The research resulted in the production of national standards of primary teachers (2002).	1990: Kroneman, M. (early years) 2001: Invargson, L.; 2002, 2008: Maloney, C.; Barblett, L.

	Statistics Canada The Research Network on New Approaches to Lifelong Learning NALL -Centre for the Study of Education and Work (CSEW), participation of Ontario Institute for Studies in Education, University of Toronto OISE/UT; The Work and Lifelong Learning Research Network WALL – grant scheme of The Social Sciences and Humanities Research Council of Canada (SSHRC)	Labor Force Survey (LFS): survey of teachers' profession: trends 1999 - 2005 – statistics: males/females, age of teachers, educational level of teachers, salaries, work load (in hours). Lifelong education: research of self-development of teachers (questionnaires, case studies). Publication: annotated bibliography.	1996–2002: NALL, 2002–2007: WALL - the Initiative for the New Economy (INE) Smaller, H. - York University; Rosemary, C. – OSSTF; Hart, D. - OISE/UT; Livingstone, D. OISE/ UT;Noormohamed, Z. York University 2006: Lin, J.
Canada	Nova Scotia Teachers Union (NSTU) Queen's University (Social Program Evaluation Group), Saint-Mary's University (Nova Scotia) Ontario Institute for Studies in Education	Research of teachers' use of time (at home, at school, their interference). Research method: diaries. Research of workload and quality of teachers' lives in Canada (Canadian Teachers' Federation). Action research and the standards of the teaching profession.	1992: King, A.J.C.; Peart, M. 2000: Harvey, A. S.; Spinney J. E. L. 2001: Schaefer, A. (British Columbia) 2005
Denmark	Aarhus Universitet -Institute of Psychology	Research of working situation of early childhood education teachers: diaries of teachers.	1979: Elklit, A.; Friis, T.
Estonia	Tallinna Ülikool	Trends of development of teachers' profession, trends in pedeutological research.	2005–2006: Ruus, V. R.; Loogma, K http: //www. ist-world.org

Finland	University of Oulu, University of Jyväskylä (in cooperation with the British University of York)	Research of early childhood education teachers: questionnaires about the practical performance of the teaching profession (1996). Comparison of approaches to professionalization of early childhood education teachers (Finland and England).	2 consecutive ethnographic research: 1994-96, 2001: Webb, R.; Vulliamy, G.; Hamalainen, S.; Sarja, A.; Kimonen, E.; Nevalainen, R.
France	ÉNS de Cachan, Institut catholique (PF); research laboratories (grants of C.N.R.S); since 1990: Universitaires de Formation des Maitres (UFMS)	De-centralized research of professionalization of teachers of primary and secondary schools	2000: Bourdoncle P.; ROBERT, A. et al.
Germany	Leibniz-Institut für die Pädagogik der Naturwissenschaften (IPN): Projekt QuiSS and GuiSS-ProSa (Professionalization of teachers' activities) Content area: sciences	Workload and working time of teachers. Professionalization of teachers – the activities of primary education teachers', development of support system and the system of evaluative methods.	1960: Frister, A.; Häker, H.;Hoppe, A. 1963: Graf, O., Rutenfranz, J. 1965: Nengelken, G.; Ulich, E. 1980: Müller-Limmroth, W, 1981: Möller, H.; Sauper, R. 1985: Häbler, H.; Kunz, A.; 1988: Wulk, J.; 1990: Schäfer, E. 1999: team-Nordrhein-Westfalen; 2001: Forneck, H. J.; Schriever, F.2004: Janzen, M. 11 schools in Schleswig-Holstein
Great Britain	BERA (British Educational Research Association in cooperation with ASPE (Association for the Study of Primary Education)	Innovations and changes in primary education – tasks, responsibilities and activities of primary school teachers, professionalization of teachers.	Webb, R. (Department of Educational Studies, University of York responsible for BERA – SIG ISCED 1 teachers'

	Cambridge University a Leicester University: Teacher Status Project	Opinions of teachers on their own profession and work, view of the public on the teaching profession, the comparison of the teachers' status and the status of other professions (e.g. research of real interactive teaching during L1 (native language) lessons, workload of teachers, practice of inclusive education, qualitative analysis of education in the context of migration, aging – ethnographical and narrative approaches). Importance for the governmental strategy of education.	2002–2006: Hargreaves, L.; McIntyre, D.; Everton, T.; Pell, T.; Hopper, B.; Rouse, M.;, Alexander, R.; Galton, M.;, Cunningham, M.; Oliver, C.
	Ofsted: Office for Standards in Education, Children's Services and Skill	Statistical research of achieving the standards according to the educational outcomes, working with disabled students, inducing novice teachers, lifelong professional education of teachers, results/success in subjects, education of minorities.	Note.: teachers' schedules at schools (curricular activities)
	Society for Educational Studies (SES)	Publishing activities focused also on the professionalization of teachers (and the research on teachers).	British Journal of Educational Studies
	The National Foundation for Educational Research	Support of educational research.	www.nfer.ac.uk
	TLRP (Teacher and Learning Research Programme), Roehampton University, King's College London)	Changing Teacher Roles, Identities and Professionalism : An Annotated Bibliography- texts on research on teachers (100 most important research studies on the status of teachers, their real life etc. in Great Britain and other countries since 2000).	2007
	Research Centre for Learning and Teaching	Research of teaching and learning.	www.ncl.ac.uk/cflat/

	VITAE project (Institute of Education, London University, University of Nottingham)	Activities and working condition of teachers' profession, their influence upon the students' performance.	
	University of Cambridge, University of Bedfordshire.	Approaches of the public to the teachers' profession – published in the collection of research reports: http://www.informaworld.com/smpp/title-content=t713707783-db=all-tab=issueslist-branches=22 - v2222, Issue 3 September 2007, p. 247 – 265.	2007: Everton, T.; Turner, P.; Hargreaves, L.; Pell, T.
	Strategic Forum for Research in Education (SFRE)	Experts' forum on research in education, including research on teachers.	www.sfre.ac.uk
	University of York UK & Finnish partner Un Yliopisto - University of Oulu, University of Jyväskylä		Also: Finland
Hungary	Debreceni Egyetem	Teachers' skills in pre-primary education: systematic and historical overview of research on teachers.	2007: Lajos, K; Pál, R., Kelemen, R.
Japan	Akita University - Faculty of Education and Human Studies Center for Educational Research and Practice, Osaka University	Research of practical teaching in schools, development of literacy (also from the point of view of clinical school psychology). Research of attitudes of teachers towards their own teaching activities connected with the reform of integrated education.	2001: Hosokawa, K.
Latvia	Kauno Technologijos Universitetas	Professiogram of primary school teachers.	1998:Tamošiūna, T. according to Čepukas
The Netherlands	Hogeschool van Am sterdam, Educatieve Hogeschool van Amsterdam	Research of new teachers' competences (method of development of scenarios in education).	2003, 2006: Snoek, M.

New Zealand	Portal Welcome to Education Counts: Teacher Status Project 2002-2006 (Ministry of education, Massey University) ICSEI - International Congress for School Effectiveness and Improvement	Statistics and educational research in New Zealand, teachers' performance (ISCED 0,1,2). Professional status of teachers (questionnaires and interviews). ICSEI – congress focused on the research of teachers' preparation, development of teachers' profession.	2002–2006: Cameron, M. Kane, R. – early childhood education 2008:ICSEI in Auckland
Norway & Sweden	Stockholm Institute of Education-Lärarhögskolan i Stockholm, Švédsko; Universitetet i Oslo	Reform policy and the performance of the teaching profession in 90ties (Scandinavia).	2008: Carlgren, I.; Klette, K.
Portugal	Universidade do Porto, Universidade de Trás-os-Montes e Alto Douro –Centre of Educational Research and Intervention (CIIE)	Professionalization of teacher's profession in comparison with other profession (90-ties) – ethnographic (sociological) research.	2007: Caria, T. H.
Saudi Arabia	King SaudUniversity, Riyadh	Comparison of target competences of primary school teachers in state schools and in private girls schools in Riyadh.	1994: Bakr Al-Bakr, F.
Slovenia	Pedagoške in andragoške raziskave pri Znanstvenem inštitutu v Ljubljane	Models of improving the quality of teachers' work in the process of professional development. Teachers' preparation, lifelong education of teachers, models of raising the quality of teachers' professional performance, reflection in teaching profession, tools of measurement of teachers' effectiveness. Research of the current state with the aim to improve the tools of measuring and raising the quality of teachers' profession.	2001–2004: Kalin, J.

Spain	Universidad Alicante, Facultade Educación	Research of learning strategies of students of teacher education via records in diaries (15-days long periods).	2004–2006: Gilar, R.; Ángeles. M. de los; Ruiz, M.; Costa, J. L. C.
Sweden	Göteborgs Universitet - centrum Research and Innovation Service See also Norway	Professional competences of teachers; theory of practical performance, relations between theory and practice in teacher education; supervision of practical training of teachers; assessment of generic skills of teachers; authenticity and self-realization of teachers; creative teacher; new demands on teachers; relations between teachers and students; educational theories in teaching practice; influence of school architecture upon the work of teachers and pupils.	Bengtsson, K.; Claesson, S.; Franke, A.; Båth, S.; Andrén, U.; Bredmar, A.C.; Johansson, J.; Lilja, A.; Levinsson, M.
Switzerland	Regional municipal offices, professional organizations and national organization of teachers ECH/ LCH –der DachverbandSchweizer Lehrerinnen und Lehrer; national research programme No. 33 SRED (Service de la Recherche en Education); CDIP/ EDK Schweizerische Konferenz der kantonalen Erziehungsdirektoren EDK Conférence suisse des directeurs cantonaux de l'instruction publique CDIP Conferenz	Further education of teachers, research of working conditions of teachers, workload of teachers.	In cantons: 1994: Fazis, U. a i.; 2000-2002 Forneck, H.J., Schriever, F., Gonik, Bucher; 2003: Trachsler, E.; Inversini, S.; Ulich, E., Wűlster, M. The whole German area: 1997/1998, 1999, 2001, 2006): Landert, Ch.

The U.S.A	AERA The American Educational Research Association, Washington	Educational research project (topics: professional development of teachers, effectiveness of teachers' preparation).	www.aera.net
	Carnegie Foundation for the Advancement of Teaching (since 1905) – independent educational research centre	Support of research activities towards the changes in education, raising the status of teachers, development of new models of reporting from practical training in classrooms, development of basic competences of teachers.	2002: Hinds, M.
	Project CLEAR	Assessment of the effectiveness of teaching according to the clarity of teachers' instructions: CLEAR = communication – learner – execution of the lesson – assessment – reflection.	70-ties.: Rosenshine & Furst, 1971, Land, 1980 a 1987, Cruickshank, Meyers, & Moenjak, 1975)
	The Holmes Group (consortium of the deans of colleges of education – approximately 100 research centres in universities		Reports on reform of teacher education

NCCTQ National Comprehensive Center for Teacher Quality: cooperation of ETS (Educational Testing Services), Learning Point Associates & Univerzity Vanderbilt	Basic empirical (statistical) research of education and quality of teachers' performance, testing in social sciences, assessment of innovativeness in education, equality of education, comparison of the level of literacy of teachers: listening, learning, leading (ETS). Purpose: the connection of research with the educational policy. Comparison of the preparation of teachers in the U. S. A. and in other countries (Australia, England, Hong Kong, Japan, Korea, the Netherlands, Singapore). Correlation between the effectiveness of the teacher and the educational outcomes (especially in economically less supported schools).	www.ncctq.org, www.ets.org
ILEARN – InternationalLeadership in Education Research Network	Network of educational research institutions.	1986, 1994: Hargreaves, A. - Lynch School of Education, Boston College
NAEd - The National Academy of Slovak and Czech Education	Educational research – national level of research. Its outcomes used in new conceptions of education with implications in practical teaching (e.g. the use of text in pre-primary education, human rights education, the life of teachers, education in areas economically underdeveloped, extra-curriculum in socio-cultural context, discrimination in education, relations teacher-students, assessing the real performance of teachers in the classroom).	since 1965
NBPTS (National Board for Professional Teaching Standards)	National standards for raising the status of teaching profession.	

NCATE National Association for the Accreditation of Teacher Education (Nebraska); INTASC (The Interstate New Teacher Assessment and Support Consortium, 1987)	Model standards for novice teachers (5 domains: the knowledge of the needs of students and the environment, the subject expertise, the ability to plan, carry out and assess one's own teaching, to prepare a diagnosis and to evaluate, what is professionalism of teachers).	www.ncate.org: deficient research of quality of teacher education
National Center for Education Statistics NCES (U.S. Department of Education, Institute of Education Sciences)	Professionalization of teachers (interest in teaching profession, working conditions, workload of teachers, commitment of teachers, profile of teachers): questionnaires of primary school teachers.	Statistical analyses„Schools &Staffing survey" 1987/88, 1990/91, 1993/84, 1997
National Center for Research on Teacher Learning	Preparation of teachers.	http://ncrtl.msu.edu
The Institute of Education Sciences, Washington D.C: Special Education Research Program on Assessment for Accountability	Project CFDA – research assessing the transparency and accountability in the area of special educational science (research of development in mathematics, writing and reading skills).	since 2005
Center for Working Families, University of California	Case studies, interviews, observations and 24-hours diaries of secondary school teachers.	2002: Barlett, L.– individual PhD research
Institute for Survey and Policy Research (University of Wisconsin-Milwaukee)	Project 'Time, work and family': working time of teachers (diaries of teachers) – every teacher carried out his/her own action research 1 day a week (Tuesday) - analysis of diaries and phone interviews.	1997-8:Drago, R.; Caplan, R.; Costanza, D.; Brubaker, T.; Cloud, D.; Harris, N.; Kashian, R.; Riggs, T. L.

US-China Center for Research on Educational Excellence	Comparative study of professional research of effectiveness of schools in the U.S.A and in China – research of correlations between the educational outcomes and the quality of education (including the teachers' input).	
Class Assignment and Teaching Assignments Study (WEAC, project STAR)	Research of problems connected with the size of classrooms, activities, assessment of their effectiveness, partially also the workload of teachers depending on the size of the classroom, stress and fluctuation of teachers.	
Design for Inquiry: Instructional Theory, Research, and Practice in Art Education	Research of the effectiveness of education (teachers' input).	Effective teacher requirements: 1983: Suydam, M., 1989: Richardson, A. G.; Arundell, A.; 1990: Young, M.
University of Wisconsin-Eau Claire, Appalachian State University, West Virginia University	Research of teachers' effectiveness (outcomes, enthusiasm, involvement of teachers).	2008: Bulger, S. M., Mohr, D. J., Walls, R.T. "Stack the Deck in Favor of Your Students by Using the Four Aces of Effective Teaching"
Competencies and Traits of Successful Agriculture Teachers	Research of teachers professional competences and features (secondary vocational education).	2007: Roberts, T.G., Dooley, K.E., Harlin, J.F., Murphrey, T. P.

Printed in the United States
By Bookmasters